Listening to Able Underachievers

Creating Opportunities for Change

Michael Pomerantz and
Kathryn Anne Pomerantz

David Fulton Publishers
London

David Fulton Publishers Ltd
The Chiswick Centre, 414 Chiswick High Road, London W4 5TF

www.fultonpublishers.co.uk

British Library Cataloguing in Publication Data
A catalogue record for this book is available from the British Library.

ISBN 1 85346 973 4

Typeset by Textype Typesetters, Cambridge
Printed in Great Britain by The Cromwell Press Ltd, Trowbridge, Wilts.

Contents

Preface

We have written this book with the intention of asking readers to accompany us on a journey of discovery, and hope that what we share with you will be of personal and professional use. It started with a long-term interest that we have in what causes some able and talented pupils in school to become less productive as learners. We call these pupils 'Able Underachievers'. We also wanted to identify what practical steps might be taken by anyone to do something constructive to minimise this waste. The topic of underachievement is of national concern, particularly in relation to pupils at Key Stage 3. As such, the stimulus material to inform the writing of this book is taken from the voices of pupils in their early teenage years. However, the points raised could easily apply to a wider age range of children and young people in education.

A cynical approach might be to argue that the complicated under-productivity problem has always been with us throughout the history of formal education. So why not just accept this fact as inevitable and concentrate our attention on those who really want to learn and to take advantage of what the school and its staff have on offer?

We feel that in the current climate this is morally, politically and economically unacceptable for many reasons and we wanted to take our project into a new area that has, historically, been under-researched, from what we have been able to ascertain. In looking at the published accounts compiled by researchers in books and academic journals there seems to be a preoccupation with what adults (mostly professional adults) think to be the causes and the solutions in respect of diminished productivity in school. The views of pupils themselves are not well recorded in the literature. Importantly, of those that we did find, there were very few examples that highlighted and developed the views of Able Underachievers themselves.

This published work was read carefully in an attempt to discover what were the key factors that were used to describe, investigate and explain the underachievement of pupils. We used these notions only as a starting point to assist us in launching our own study.

Quantitative research methods have traditionally been used to gather information in the form of statistical data for comparative purposes. These methods are still widely used as seen, for example, in the acquisition of National Curriculum attainment figures (SATs) and the publication of school league tables. Many educators would argue that this methodology is insufficiently sensitive to expose the underlying reasons for underachievement.

An analogy might be given to the study of shadows. If you want to know more about a shadow, it is unlikely that the application of a strong searchlight on the subject will shed much new 'light' or depth of understanding on the subject in question. A lamp is too crude and intrusive. It does not respect the subtlety and the vulnerability of the shadow that you wanted to investigate in the first place. To study a shadow or some other sensitive topic effectively would require the use of a different approach. The ideological and political revolution favouring more inclusion in all aspects of our lives has stimulated a process that is giving us insights that were previously hidden. There is greater interest today in the use of qualitative research methods which are designed to probe and capture the voices, thoughts, feelings and ideas of people traditionally under-represented in published studies.

Social scientists have tried to access difficult material by using questionnaires and by interviewing people called subjects to see what can be learned. Some investigators use very restricted questions in order to be more objective and perhaps scientific, but of late, greater interest is developing in taking a listening approach, in which the material to be studied is actually a dialogue between the curious adult and the person whose opinions are being sought. The authors sought to use these methods to listen to the opinions of Able Underachievers.

In this book we hope to share with you what we have discovered and what we think and feel about it. It has been a great privilege to ask pupils to tell us what they believe to be their responses to questions raised by adults in our effort to understand underachievement. Before putting this into book form we took the results and our interpretations and summaries of those results to a number of individuals and audiences to gauge their reactions and further clarify where we wanted to take the project in its next phase. Their responses have helped to bring life to the report in its printed version. Appreciation for their contributions is noted. Readers are asked to accept our presupposition that what these Able Underachievers have said does not necessarily reflect the views of the entire population of Able Underachievers.

In the future, we hope to engage a handful of other pupil and teacher groups in replicating and extending our study in their own schools, in the hopes that by doing their own investigations they would be more inclined to want to follow up suggestions for change than if they were exclusively dependent on the opinions of outsiders.

As authors we have also had the experience ourselves of being pupils, parents, teachers, trainers, managers, researchers and educational psychologists. We can, therefore, bring our own qualities and perceptions to bear on the subject of ability and underachievement. What any researcher will tell you is that there are pitfalls in setting out on an investigation, in that the methodology and instruments used are heavily influenced by our prior experiences and expectations of what we hope to demonstrate.

Further to this, we are living in an age of accountability which brings with it an increasing amount of pressure, not just on parents and professionals but also on pupils themselves. If we allow ourselves to become immersed in the inevitable amount of stress and competition that these pressures can bring to bear we can soon lose sight of what it means to enjoy learning and the power and gain associated with healthy collaboration. To be successful, collaboration is very much dependent on the emotional health of individuals and organisations and on the need to have sustainable, facilitative communication between all the parties involved. These are significant factors to bear in mind if we are serious about tackling underachievement.

Underachievement, in general terms, is inextricably linked with social and emotional factors, and yet the vast majority of books aimed at supporting the needs of able pupils are invested in the area of curriculum development. Those existing texts that do make reference to the social and emotional needs of Able Underachievers tend to be written from the perspectives of educators, but with some recognition of the need to redress the balance:

> . . . as the momentum of the debate increases and far-reaching decisions begin to be made about the needs of the gifted and talented, we ought to pause and consider perhaps the most important perspective of all – the views of the children themselves. We can then, at least, begin to lay claim to having addressed needs as part of the process of meeting them. (Stopper 2000: 124)

The purpose of this book has been to study the views of Able Underachievers in secondary schools and identify real possibilities for change. In the research study that inspired the writing of this book, the authors began with a list of ideas or constructs they identified through their own experience and reading of the literature as having been hypothesised as key initial factors influencing Able Underachievers. The authors felt that strong influences would relate to teaching and learning factors, peer group factors and family factors. Analysis of the views of the Able Underachievers themselves did confirm that there were influencing factors in all three areas, but in view of the perspectives of the pupils questioned, the original list of constructs needed to be significantly modified to reflect the overwhelming evidence that factors directly related to the learning environment made the greatest impact on the underachievement of those pupils.

Edward de Bono, in his book *New Thinking for the New Millennium* (de Bono 1999), claims that we have become a nation of analysts constantly searching for the truth. As researchers we did not want to fall into the trap of drawing conclusions about underachievement that might add further to the current debate and leave it at that. Our main purpose was to look for a real opportunity to engage in synthesis and to design a means of creating a cultural shift towards increased levels of achievement in our schools. This revolutionary approach involves the active participation of all stakeholders interested in turning the potential of our able pupils into performance.

The Able Underachievers in our study, to whom we are indebted for giving us the gift of their time and honesty, demonstrated their skills in oracy and humility, and also provided us with clues which increased our understanding of under-achievement generally. If Able Underachievers themselves can be instrumental in creating change, our vision is that this change will be reflected in the achievements of all pupils. The real purpose of this book is, therefore, about empowerment and opportunity. We hope that the content will be of interest, in particular to teachers and others who will find in its pages the inspiration for change. We strongly believe that high achievers are made not born and, therefore, we as adults have a responsibility for the making of more enlightened and enlivened future generations.

Michael and Kathryn Anne Pomerantz
March 2002

Acknowledgements

The work in this book represents a collaboration between the young people interviewed, their teachers, those who read and commented upon earlier drafts, those who responded within workshops offering advice and suggestions and ourselves. We must assume responsibility for the final version but we want to extend our thanks and appreciation to all those who helped us.

Special thanks go to Ann Locke, Joyce Scaife, John Gallagher and David Thompson for helping us to shape our thoughts along the way and to other friends and colleagues for their valued editorial comments.

This book was inspired by and is dedicated to our parents: Betty and Mihiel Pomerantz and Janet and Nigel Pollard.

CHAPTER 1

Introduction to the study of Able Underachievers

Purpose of the book

This book is based on the exploration of what the authors found when they questioned a group of Able Underachieving teenagers to elicit their views as to why Able Underachievers underperform at secondary school, and what they think can be done to reduce this underachievement.

We suspect that underachievement is an expensive problem that thus far has never been satisfactorily measured or understood in terms of its extent and the social costs to the school, to the larger community and ultimately to the economy and the life of the nation. Wills and Munro (2000) suggest that 10–15 per cent of intellectually able students are underachievers. Whybra (2000) argues that probably over 50 per cent of gifted students work in school four or five years below their ability. If the level of underachievement is so extensive, then it suggests that the problem needs to be investigated and tackled systematically. We often hear the expression 'a mind is a terrible thing to waste'. We owe this investigation not just to the nation but to the individual children and young people who enter the educational system with innocence and trust.

If we discover ways of improving the situation for Able Underachievers in school there ought to be a dividend that will benefit a wider cross-section of the school population. Teaching that is more responsive to the needs of Able Underachievers could well be appropriate for less able students as a positive side-effect. For example, in schools that make good provision for their most able pupils, provision for pupils with special educational needs is also found to be good (Eyre 1997).

In presenting these findings to several professional audiences, we were told repeatedly that the suggestions made by our respondents would be widely applicable and that most pupils, rather than just Able Underachievers, would benefit from changes at school.

Background

Before starting to write this book we had already become familiar with much of the published literature in the field of able students and we had noted that the language used was definitely more characteristic of what adult professionals write than what teenagers might be inclined to offer by way of partial explanations to account for underachievement. Here are some paraphrased examples to convey the flavour of adult language:

- Able Underachievers are not adequately motivated by teachers in the classroom;
- the curriculum is inappropriate for Able Underachievers;
- the government does not invest enough in resources or training for teachers;
- the peer group culture is too strong and pulls Able Underachievers away from hard effort;
- Able Underachievers want to avoid being singled out for attention or praise for their accomplishments;
- the media is to blame as it does not celebrate pupil achievements adequately;
- parents have failed to instil an adequate achievement ethic in their Able Underachievers;
- some teachers are not up to the task of inspiring Able Underachievers to work to their potential; and
- everyone is out to blame someone else for the problem and its lack of resolution.

This last point involves a circular and counter-productive pattern of social blame, and ignores the contribution that Able Underachievers themselves could make to the debate if one is to be convened. Where is this debate being held today? The voices of Able Underachievers, individually and collectively, are not well documented in the literature. This book tries to redress the balance.

Definitions of Able Underachievers

We do not intend to dwell long on complicated notions about who (exactly or technically) Able Underachievers are, as this could be protracted and would detract from our main purpose which is to describe the plight of a group of able underachieving pupils who are not receiving a fair share of the educational provision on offer in schools today. Perhaps they never have. Notions of 'definition' are well documented elsewhere.

It is worth noting that the House of Commons Select Committee (1999) enquiry into the education of highly able children was unable to identify an agreed definition of able pupils or the size of the sub-population that constitutes able pupils. Despite looking at a large amount of evidence, no consensus was reached on these matters. We did not want to repeat this exercise here. It is well known that many Able Underachievers are hard to identify (Teare 1997). Among those educators most prominent in the field there was a shift in emphasis around 1998–99 towards the view that identification is best established through making provision. For example, if teachers were to include more challenging tasks in the classroom for all students, the most able might become apparent more by the way they approach the challenge than by teachers merely identifying a cohort based on outcomes or achievements.

As a starting point we might consider that Able Underachievers are those pupils in school who could be gaining marks or grades like As or Bs on assessments of their work when in fact they tend to be achieving Cs or below. In terms of the National Curriculum and predicted functioning on the SATs at the end of Key Stage 3, we are talking of pupils who are capable of performing above Level 6 (in some subjects) but whom staff believe will not be likely to achieve this standard. We are specifically talking of the pupils in the top third of the student talent pool in terms of 'potential', but whose performance as assessed or measured in school does not generally reflect this.

Among the top third of the talent pool there is an indeterminate number of pupils who are Able Underachievers. There is great scope to argue about the size and the potential impact of this group in schools. We could arbitrarily agree on a defining standard such as a particular measure or test of potential, and then likewise arbitrarily agree on another defining measure or test of attainment. Having completed this quantitative task we could again arbitrarily (for the third time) determine mathematically a cut-off point to use for dividing the talented group into subsets called 'Able Underachievers' and 'Able Achievers' within the top third of the student population.

Later, another team of researchers would use different criteria or measures to do basically the same job and publish their findings. Later still, another research team would spot the difference in the findings and the size of the Able Underachievers' subgroups. General readers among the public then would be left (predictably) with the time-honoured problem of watching an educational debate spiral out of control, leaving little advance in our collective understanding of the needs of Able Underachievers. We sought a different approach to the problem.

Measurement

Elsewhere, readers could study the intricacies of the methodological problems facing researchers who try to measure human activity such as potential or attainment or discrepancies, in order to enhance research. The debates have raged for years. At one extreme, proponents of formal assessment argue positively about the rigour employed in testing large groups of individuals, which they feel results in stable, valid and reliable data upon which to draw assumptions and make predictions. At the other end of the continuum, equally convincing arguments suggest that tests of 'potential' are too narrow and ought instead to capture multiple intelligences (Gardner 1993), assuming that new instruments can be developed to measure this, although this is not proving to be an easy task. We should also perhaps try to assess a broad range of skills including, for example, leadership and social awareness that would be difficult to quantify (Ogilvie 1973). Still others emphasise further methodological problems or biases with testing on the basis of ethnicity, social class, gender or even reading skills among the test takers (Wallace 2000).

Selection process

We were impatient in this current study to move on rather than to await the outcome of the long-standing debate which we have just outlined.

Our work took place within one large, predominantly rural, local education authority (LEA). We decided to ask the head teachers or their representatives in 11 randomly chosen secondary schools to select or nominate Able Underachievers who could subsequently be interviewed in order to hear their perspectives. To facilitate this process we offered school staff four staged criteria in the selection process, knowing elements of error might be introduced in the selection as we lacked a universally agreed rule for Able Underachiever subject selection. Subsequent analyses showed that the schools randomly selected were not significantly different from the rest of the secondary schools in the LEA on several comparative measures such as GCSE results, social deprivation (free school meals index) and school size. This showed that the randomisation procedure had been effective and that the selected schools were not statistically different from the other schools in those areas where comparative measures were used.

Staged criteria

The staged criteria through which school staff were asked to draw up a list of potential interview candidates are listed in Appendix 1. From this list, interviewees were randomly chosen. In the end, we selected 26 Year 9 pupils to interview. This year group was targeted because of significant educational concerns regarding underachievement at Key Stage 3.

The 26 Able Underachievers, finally identified after the four stages were applied, constituted the interviewee group of volunteers where parental permission for interviews had been granted, and the selection process stopped. There were five girls and 21 boys in the interviewee cohort. None of those interviewed were from an ethnic minority group despite an earlier request to head teachers that both female students and pupils from ethnic minorities be represented in the sample selected. There is a need for future research to further explore underachievement in relation both to girls and pupils from ethnic minority groups.

Early constructs

Before we began the task of finding Able Underachievers to interview we had to give considerable thought as to what to ask them. Questionnaires as a research tool had been considered but rejected as we wanted to obtain the richness and depth that only comes from face-to-face semi-structured conversations. Questioning techniques range from highly specific items (where the researcher knows exactly what he or she wants answered and how) to really open-ended probes where the researcher wants to avoid leading or influencing the interviewee too heavily. We chose a compromise in which we studied the language and the ideas in some of the published literature before compiling a list of 36 open-ended questions.

The task of writing appropriate, semi-structured, oral questions to ask Able Underachievers about their underachievement in the search both for causation and remedy began with an overview of what others had contributed in published reports over the years. A trawl through the literature about able, gifted or talented pupils produced a huge list of constructs or dimensions from which the authors produced a series of interview questions. It was hoped that this might have some bearing on the processes underlying underachievement. Table 1.1 provides a list of possible constructs influencing achievement and underachievement that came from this trawl.

The language in the table is that of adults rather than teenage pupils, with a lot of psychology underlying the constructs. Using this list as a starting point, very general or open-ended questions were drafted and then subjected to two separate pilot interview exercises to assess their suitability, accessibility and usefulness. Questions that appeared ambiguous, confusing or redundant were revised or omitted. The interviews were planned to last about 20–30 minutes.

In the end the authors decided to use the list of questions or probes in Table 1.2 below to begin a conversation, with follow-up questioning to take place where it seemed natural and appropriate in order to extract the greatest meaning from the interviewee's perspective.

Interview procedure

The pupils were interviewed individually in a small quiet room in their own school at a mutually agreed time. Sessions lasted from 20 to 30 minutes on average. The interviews took place during the summer term of 2000.

After a brief introduction with reassurances about the research project and confidentiality, the planned 36 questions were administered with follow-up

Table 1.1 Constructs possibly influencing achievement and underachievement

Positive or facilitating factors	Negative or debilitating factors
Anxiety (positive)	Anxiety (negative)
Aspirations (high)	Aspirations (low)
Attribution (internal)	Attribution (external)
Boredom (low)	Boredom (high)
Challenge appropriate	Challenge inappropriate
Competition helps	Competition hinders
Concentration good	Concentration weak
Confidence strong	Confidence weak
Conformity fosters achievement	Conformity hinders achievement
Culture: success is comfortable	Culture: success is not comfortable
Curriculum appropriate	Curriculum inappropriate
Dependency (low)	Dependency (high)
External reinforcement	External punishment
Fears are constructive	Fears are not constructive
Fear of failure (low)	Fear of failure (high)
Identity established	Identity not established
Learning model (adult)	Learning model (child)
Mentor available	Mentor not available
Mistakes promote learning	Mistakes interfere with learning
Motivation (high)	Motivation (low)
Needs met	Needs unmet
Opportunities are present	Opportunities are absent
Parent attitudes (positive)	Parent attitudes (negative)
Parent behaviour (positive)	Parent behaviour (negative)
Parent expectations (positive)	Parent expectations (negative)
Parent pressure (positive)	Parent pressure (negative)
Peer attitudes (positive)	Peer attitudes (negative)
Peer behaviour (positive)	Peer behaviour (negative)
Peer expectations (positive)	Peer expectations (negative)
Peer pressure (positive)	Peer pressure (negative)
Persistence (high)	Persistence (low)
Pupil culture and social world = (positive)	Pupil culture and social world = (negative)
Repetition infrequent	Repetition excessive
Research skills developed	Research skills under-developed
Responsibility (high)	Responsibility (low)
Risk taking (positive)	Risk taking (negative)
Role models (positive)	Role models (negative)
Self-discipline established	Self-discipline missing

Self-esteem (high)	Self-esteem (low)
Self-assessment (high)	Self-assessment (low)
Setting high standards	Setting low standards
Sibling attitudes (positive)	Sibling attitudes (negative)
Sibling behaviour (positive)	Sibling behaviour (negative)
Sibling expectations (positive)	Sibling expectations (negative)
Sibling pressure (positive)	Sibling pressure (negative)
Teacher attitudes (positive)	Teacher attitudes (negative)
Teacher behaviour (positive)	Teacher behaviour (negative)
Teacher expectations (positive)	Teacher expectations (negative)
Teacher pressure (positive)	Teacher pressure (negative)
Teamwork (positive)	Teamwork (negative)
Time management (positive)	Time management (negative)

Table 1.2 Interview schedule

Curriculum
1. What gives you a buzz or excitement in and out of school?
2. What turns you off or bores you in or out of school?
3. When do you find the work really demanding in school? (Elaborate)
4. Have you ever had the opportunity to join an interesting activity or group either in or outside of school? (Elaborate)
5. If something really interested or excited you in school how would you develop this?
Attributes
6. Tell me what your favourite teachers are like.
7. What do some teachers do that causes you to dislike them?
Influences
8. What do your teachers do to encourage or discourage your progress in school?
(Probe if necessary)
Who do you live with at home? (Background question)
9. What do your parent(s) [or carer(s)] do to encourage or discourage your progress in school?
(Probe if necessary)
10. Tell me about the other pupils that you like to spend time with. What are they like?
11. What do other pupils do to encourage or discourage your progress in school?
(Probe if necessary)
12. Would your friends say the same thing?

13. Do your brothers or sisters exert any influence on your work and if so how?

14. In this school what do your friends think about clever pupils?

[If the response is negative probe for reasons and interventions to change attitudes.]

15. How often do you feel there is a conflict of interest between advice from your teachers and your friends?

Self

16. What do you like about yourself?

17. What do you dislike about yourself?

18. Do you think that worrying interferes with your learning in school? [Probe for examples]

19. What characteristics do you feel you possess that are not valued by your teachers, friends, or parents?

20. Do you believe that you are not really working up to your ability?

[If 'Yes,'] How do you know this?

21. What do you do differently from other students in school who achieve at a higher level than you do?

22. Do you think in general that you are good at learning?

23. How do you know that?

Interventions

24. How do you learn best?

25. Have you developed your own study skills? [If 'Yes'] What are they?

26. What do you do when you are bored or not engaged that helps to get you back to serious work?

27. Does this tend to work?

28. What would make you work harder?

29. If you were to design a new school courses and ways of teaching it that would inspire you, what would it be like?

30. Imagine that your teachers want you to do A. Your friends want you to do B instead. Think of an example. What do you usually do?

31. If you were studying underachievement what question would you ask students? . . . I'd like you to answer your own question.

32. Are the standards set for you high enough?

33. Who would you be inclined to blame for your underachievement?

34. On average how much time do you spend on homework each night?

35. Do you have any plans to attend college or university later in life?

36. If I were to come back and see you in a year would the situation have changed? Would you be working harder?

questioning as and where appropriate. The intent was to gather as much information as possible from the interviewees in their individual responses. All sessions were tape recorded and subsequently transcribed by a typist who was unaware of the design or scope of the research project.

A sample of the transcripts was compared with the original tape recordings and a very high degree of accuracy was noted. There were very few situations where what was recorded could not be transcribed, such as when there was unanticipated background noise. The pilot exercise had showed us that it was important to attend to noise levels outside the interview room. Readers interested in the intricacies of just how the authors used the transcribed textual statements captured within interviews can see the material in Appendix 2. Some readers might want a more detailed record of just how this was done and the software application (ATLAS.ti) that was used. This can also be found in Appendix 2. For many, however, there may be even greater curiosity at this stage to understand the researchers' analysis of what the 26 Able Underachievers actually said rather than how their words were coded and stored for easier retrieval.

Outcomes

The key constructs that emerged from the Able Underachievers themselves are further refined and presented as a new list of constructs (Table 1.3) influencing underachievers, which replaces the initial list from which the original questions for the interviews were based. The original list contained 51 constructs which have now been reduced to 25. Comparison of the original and revised lists of constructs reveals that the Able Underachievers' responses were predominantly centred on the teaching environment and to a lesser extent on the influence of peers and lesser still to family influences. The trend in these findings mirrors that found by O'Grady (1995) who investigated the underachievement of pupils in junior high school. The authors, on the basis of their reading of the literature, had originally included far more constructs relating to peers and family relationships, predicting these to be strong influencing factors.

The new constructs were subdivided into those relating to: 'communication and relationships', 'teaching and learning' and 'personal and emotional factors'. Note that those with an asterix (*) were in the original list. The revised list is more specific and enables us now to move beyond the analysis to considering each area of influence in depth.

The reader can perhaps empathise with the following constructs highlighted as facilitating and debilitating by the Able Underachievers. The exception to this would in the authors' view be the construct of 'Peer Affiliation' (marked in italics in Table 1.3) in which it was generally found to be the case that the Able Underachievers did not want to associate with Able Achievers and in many cases would see this as undesirable. No Able Underachiever stated that he or she felt that affiliation with an Able Achiever in school would facilitate his or her progress. The authors consider this to be a lost opportunity. However, Able Underachievers generally were happy to seek support from older able siblings. O'Grady (1995) also found this to be the case and, when questioned, the Able Underachievers in her study said they would not feel embarrassed in asking for help at home, but they would in front of their peers. On the surface of it one might conclude from this that the peer group is responsible for the culture that exists in which Able Underachievers do not affiliate in learning contexts with Able Achievers. Yet, if the learning environment was engineered to be more psychologically safe, nurturing and collaborative, opportunities for the two able pupil groups (Able Achievers and Able Underachievers) to affiliate with each other, could be established.

Table 1.3 Constructs influencing Able Underachievers (revised list)

Positive or facilitating factors	Negative or debilitating factors
Communication and relationships	**Communication and relationships**
Teacher explanation (clear)	Teacher explanation (unclear)
Teacher–pupil respect (high)	Teacher–pupil respect (low)
Teacher–pupil interaction (positive)	Teacher–pupil interaction (negative)
Teacher questioning (open)	Teacher questioning (closed)
Teacher expectations (positive) (*)	Teacher expectations (negative) (*)
Pupil classroom talk (academic)	Pupil classroom talk (social)
Parent and teacher feedback (positive)	Parent and teacher feedback (negative)
Teaching and learning	**Teaching and learning**
Classroom environment (relaxed)	Classroom environment (stressed)
Classroom activities (fun)	Classroom activities (tedious)
Curriculum emphasis (practical)	Curriculum emphasis (traditional)
Teaching style (diverse)	Teaching style (didactic)
School values (risk-taking)	School values (conformity)
Enrichment activities (included)	Enrichment activities (absent)
Rewards and incentives (more apparent)	Rewards and incentives (less apparent)
Pupil skills and interests (acknowledged)	Pupil skills and interests (unidentified)
Collaboration (encouraged)	Collaboration (discouraged)
Personal and emotional	**Personal and emotional**
Adult power base (democratic)	Adult power base (autocratic)
Parent and teacher support (high)	Parent and teacher support (low)
Sibling behaviour (helpful)	Sibling behaviour (unhelpful)
Peer affiliation (average/less able pupils)	*Peer affiliation (Able Achievers)*
Locus of control (internal)	Locus of control (external)
Study skills (diverse)	Study skills (limited)
Motivation (high) (*)	Motivation (low) (*)
Boredom (low) (*)	Boredom (high) (*)
Concentration (good) (*)	Concentration (weak) (*)

The next four chapters present the key outcomes of this study that emerged as the following themes:

- teachers communicating with Able Underachievers;
- developing relationships with peers, siblings and parents;
- thinking and learning with Able Underachievers; and
- responding to personal and emotional needs.

For each key outcome, evidence is provided directly from the young people themselves which is subject to a degree of interpretation and analysis by the authors. The readers should bear in mind that these are the commonly held views of the pupils themselves. Both authors having taught and raised children themselves are aware of how easily dismissive or defensive one could be in hearing these messages. Following this, a range of possible solutions is explored and developed in the form of practical suggestions and ideas for creating opportunities for change.

Throughout the text, readers will encounter many invitations to reflect on their own practices and experiences. Of course, readers may choose not to engage interactively with the text, but in making this choice, they may find, by the time they reach the concluding chapter, that declining these invitations is a further example of lost opportunities, a theme highlighted by the Able Underachievers in the study. The readers could, of course, choose to return to earlier sections of the text, but the authors would stress that, if the readers are seriously wishing to be instrumental in creating change themselves, they would gain more from engaging actively with the text from the outset.

Suggestions for further reading

The procedure for analysing what the Able Underachievers said involved a grounded theory approach requiring the reading of each line of each transcript and the coding of selected segments in order to be able to keep track of recurring themes throughout the exercise. Further details about the method can be found in:

Miles, M. B. and Huberman, A. M. (1994) *Qualitative Data Analysis: A source book of new methods.*
Strauss, A. L. and Corbin, J. (1998) *Basics of Qualitative Research: Techniques and procedures for developing grounded theory (2nd edn).*

CHAPTER 2

Teachers communicating with Able Underachievers

In any aspect of life, if something is not going to plan then one strategy is to use language to talk about it. If we relate this to Able Underachievers, then we need to consider the conversations that can take place between teacher, parent and pupil to address the issue. In this chapter the authors highlight and interpret the key comments that the Able Underachievers made regarding the influence of the communications they have with their teachers that affect their academic progress. Opportunities for improving communication with Able Underachievers are explored. The pupils' responses indicate that the way in which adults communicate with Able Underachievers has a marked effect on their willingness to engage in the learning process. See Figure 2.1 below.

- Able Underachievers value good relations with friendly, attentive, available, respectful, socially skilful teachers with a sense of humour, with whom they can communicate in a more adult fashion thus avoiding the 'cat and mouse' roles that prevent real dialogue. Unfortunately, they feel this is rare at school.
- They dislike unfair, boring, shouting, stressed, overly critical, disorganised and unassertive teachers. They are pessimistic about improvements and feel no sense of problem ownership. They are not in dialogue with anyone to repair the situation.
- They feel that teachers are influential in that they can stimulate or kill interest and enthusiasm. Much depends on teachers' abilities to use language in the classroom in ways that are clear, concise and encouraging. Some teachers themselves may not recognise that they have the power to increase motivation and attainment by changing some of the ways in which they communicate with pupils.
- They are bored by teachers who talk too much in class and who do not explain clearly.

Figure 2.1 Key research outcomes specific to the theme of the way teachers communicate that influences Able Underachievers

What the pupils said about their favourite teachers

Q6. Tell me what your favourite teachers are like.

This question was used to identify the behaviours, characteristics and attributes of valued teachers of Able Underachievers. It is the first in a series of questions designed to assess the influence that teachers among others might have over the work of their pupils. To some extent the findings are probably typical of what most Year 9 pupils in general would say, although the authors did not collect data that might reflect the views of pupils generally. Able Underachievers like and appear to value teachers who are:

- friendly
- cheerful
- funny
- understanding
- tolerant
- balanced

- assertive
- non-sexist
- fair
- not overly critical
- unstressed
- helpful

- good listeners
- encouraging
- available
- good at explaining
- attentive
- focused

At least seven pupils (27 per cent) specifically and spontaneously mentioned liking teachers who do not shout. This seemed to be a remarkably high number of responses targeting just one single aspect of what teachers might choose to do or not do. There were repeated references to appreciating adults who have a sense of humour and who will tell jokes. Pupils acknowledged appreciation for teachers who allow pupils to talk at appropriate times rather than having to endure excessive periods of silence.

Subject 5: If you are stuck you ask for help and they help and they explain it to you and if you are still unsure they'll wait until you know what you are doing before they tell you to do it; they make sure you know what you are doing. They don't watch over you all the time. They give you a bit of space and freedom like, for example, art. They don't tell you exactly what you've got to do . . . like if you need help they are there but if you don't need it then they don't.

Interviewer: Is there anything else she does that would make her a favourite teacher?

Subject 13: Erm she's always there to help if you ever need anything.

Subject 13: She'll explain things like over and over again in different like forms that you'd be able to explain to anyone else in totally different forms but without it getting boring going over and over it again.

Interpretation

Some of the Able Underachievers allude to feeling the benefits of attentiveness and mutual respect between teacher and pupil in a more grown-up or adult manner of communication. While this is infrequent, it raises questions as to what we can do to encourage more of this in the hopes of raising the aspirations and performance of Able Underachievers. The accolade of hearing a pupil say *she's always there* is worthy of further consideration as a desirable attribute in the teaching profession. How to achieve this is another matter, but the process can start with an acknowledgement that some teachers manage to communicate this message of availability to their students better than others.

In other words, these Able Underachievers might well be able to communicate in a more adult-like manner with better dialogue and exchange of meaning than might be expected if we looked only at predictions based on the written work they submit in school. The Able Underachievers might well be able to enter a better planned learning conversation with some teaching staff in a manner or a forum that currently either does not exist or does so only fleetingly. None of the Able Underachievers interviewed had an interesting, spontaneous story to tell about a singularly important conversation held with a teacher in school on the very subject of underachievement, its causes and its remedies.

Why is this shown to be true in the texts of 26 individual interviews? Why are the principal characters in this evolving story not really talking to one another on a meaningful basis? Is it a profound lack of trust in one another? Is it that a busy classroom teacher feels there is no time to do this, or that it is a pastoral responsibility that should be undertaken by another staff member? Is it about sticking to an obsolete teacher–pupil script? Is it a matter of waiting to see who makes the first move? Is it about a history of arrested pupil–teacher conversations which are not balanced and reinforce the power differentials between the participants? Is it merely a 'cat and mouse' game that avoids moving into new territory that could benefit all parties? Are participants unaware of the conversation that might be possible? Are they trapped in a non-conversation, feeling too discouraged to try out a new script?

Questions for the reader

How do you feel about what Able Underachievers are telling us?

Do you agree with what the Able Underachievers are saying?

Have you seen any evidence of this for yourself?

Is there any value in the messages from Able Underachievers to us?

Is there anything readers could do in response to Able Underachievers' words?

What the pupils said about the causes of disliking some teachers

Q7. What do some teachers do that causes you to dislike them?
This question continues the theme of teachers' influence. Able Underachievers are quick to describe what their teachers actually do that reduces student interest and attention. They do not like teachers who are:

- unfair
- inclined to shout (seven adverse comments here)
- overly critical
- poor at explaining
- inclined not to listen to them
- boring
- seeming to pick on pupils
- too talkative
- frustrating
- on your back
- frequently nagging and complaining
- observed embarrassing other pupils
- seen to single out pupils inappropriately
- known to have favourites or pets
- inclined to exaggerate their own importance
- perceived as using put-downs

Interpretation

It seems unlikely that either experienced teachers or teachers in training are unfamiliar with this predictable list of complaints about teachers that are out of favour with students in general. It is quite likely that teachers would want to avoid being seen by a colleague or an Ofsted inspector engaging in any of these unfortunate behaviours. Yet our sample of Able Underachievers suggest in individual interviews that these same bad habits or practices continue to occur in schools to the detriment of student progress.

Once again we hear the voices of a disenchanted cohort speaking out confidently in individual interviews as if to a newspaper reporter who might well be naïve about current school-based practice and might not know how damaging these teachers' behaviours can be. The Able Underachievers were not stuck or confused when asked about this. They were able to recite chapter and verse as evidence to substantiate their claims that some of the ways some teachers relate to their pupils has a part to play in the subsequent underachievement. Is this inevitable?

There was little revolutionary sign that the Able Underachievers felt they owned a stake in the problem and wanted to initiate legitimate and socially appropriate action to improve their circumstances at school. There was an inevitable quality to their reports as if nothing would be likely to change. They certainly were not competing for a leadership role in reforming schooling. In an era where excluded and disadvantaged minorities all over the world are finding ways to express themselves, this Able Underachiever cohort seemed quite resigned to accepting the *status quo* as if it were not their problem and were content to sit back and endure it for the time being. Again this is a lost opportunity for those wanting to raise standards in schools. It would be encouraging to see more evidence of their voices being expressed and heard.

Questions for the reader

Why do you suppose that these pupils do not feel the problem has much to do with themselves?

Why are they not more angry or motivated to do something?

Is it learned helplessness or indifference?

Is this a cultural factor?

Would they say the effort required to change the situation is excessive and unreasonable?

Do you think that some teachers are unaware that the way in which they relate to some pupils has such a negative effect on pupil motivation and achievement?

What could be done to address this?

If Able Underachievers would own some of the underachievement problem instead of attributing blame for the problem to some teachers they then might feel more empowered to see what steps they could take to do something positive. Able Underachievers could make a positive gesture themselves and make their intentions clear to teachers, who might be so impressed with the possibilities that they themselves might subsequently change their own behaviours with the result of a vastly improved classroom environment. Everyone could therefore win. When Paulo Freire wrote the *Pedagogy of the Oppressed* (1970), he argued convincingly that those looking for change in education should focus on the disenfranchised rather than on those perceived as holding power.

What the pupils said about teachers influencing Able Underachievers

Q8. What do your teachers do to encourage or discourage your progress in school?

This was perhaps a complicated question where frequent follow-up was required, especially in cases where pupils mentioned something positive about teachers being encouraging but forgot to say anything about teachers being discouraging. The authors wanted to see how influential teachers were perceived in the underachievement of this group of Able Underachiever students. It was also interesting to see whether the respondents wanted to start with an emphasis on praise or criticism and whether their analysis was balanced. In the end, the authors received a mixed collection of views.

Responses were very varied from the extreme of associating most accomplishments and underachievement with teachers' attributes and behaviours to not seeing a clear influential link between what teachers do and how Able Underachievers respond. Able Underachievers obviously value teachers:

- encouraging progress by, for example, asking good questions
- stimulating interest
- encouraging hard effort
- being responsive
- making lessons fun
- utilising humour
- rewarding good work and effort
- being practical
- establishing good control and discipline in the classroom
- setting high expectations and standards
- enlivening lessons
- being warm
- reporting positive news to parents
- acknowledging talent
- making the work exciting

Teachers can discourage progress amongst Able Underachievers by:

- being boring
- using unnecessary repetition
- killing interest
- showing preferential treatment to favourites or pets
- being overly negative
- being overly directive
- setting inappropriate standards
- missing opportunities to be helpful or offer praise
- punishing inappropriately
- picking on some pupils unfairly and embarrassing them
- holding an exaggerated sense of their own status
- not listening at times

There is considerable overlap between the above characteristics and those identified in response to the two previous questions. This confirms their significance as far as the pupils themselves are concerned.

A few Able Underachievers spoke with great affection for their teachers. Some could explain how teachers use preparation and charisma to bring life into the classroom while other Able Underachievers seemed unsure about how to account for the successful methods used by their teachers. Note this example:

Subject 13: Erm there's Mr S . . . he's my English teacher and, erm the best one I've probably had so far. He's extremely funny and he makes it fun to learn and he's just . . . erm . . . there's jokes every lesson, but then he turns on this serious side and everyone has had a laugh and everything so we'll work really hard . . . say if we were doing, erm like advertising like and he let us like choose what we wanted to do and we chose to all like do an advert and I had a funny based one and we were all doing it and everything and then he comes in and like helps us all with . . . while having a laugh at the same time and after he'd gone he was having a laugh and everything but we'd also learnt like how to make it like a lot better without realising unless you actually stop and think about it you didn't realise what you'd done.

Interpretation

Teaching is very much a performing art that develops with practice. Some teachers are gifted, charismatic, influential and serve as catalysts for high level standards among their pupils. When this happens everyone benefits. Pupils do not always understand the method and the motives underlying what teachers offer in the classroom but they can spot good teaching and they value it and they are quite skilful at conveying their appreciation and admiration for good teaching.

When this does not occur spontaneously Able Underachievers are inclined to sit back passively and withhold their own considerable talents, inventiveness, leadership and other contributions that might tip the balance toward success. Probably this is because the strong adolescent culture confirms that the classroom is the responsibility of the teacher, and Able Underachievers are not expected to use their skills either to rescue or repair failing lessons or to be an ally to a teacher in need of social support. This is true whether this is consciously acknowledged or not by the teacher.

Q2. What turns you off or bores you in or out of school?

This question relates more to learning factors and is analysed in more detail in Chapter 4. However, in responding to this question, Able Underachievers referred to the amount and quality of teacher talk in classrooms:

Subject 6: When people talk for too long, when teachers talk too much.

Subject 2: Teachers going on and on and not doing anything exciting they just keep going on and you lose interest after about five minutes.

Interviewer: Some teachers do this?

Subject 2: Yer they just talk and go on . . . and they mumble as well.

What can be done by teachers to improve communication with Able Underachievers?

The two most significant themes suggested by the Able Underachievers themselves were firstly, the desire to be heard by teachers who are friendly and take a personal interest in them and secondly, their need to experience teachers who are skilled at

---

Questions for the reader

As a reader are you yet able to identify with Able Underachievers as fellow human beings either from your own personal experience or from witnessing Able Underachievers in classes?

If you could return to the classroom and talk with these Able Underachievers what might you ask them yourselves?

Would you have any advice to offer them?

Is the situation really as gloomy and pessimistic as they describe in some lessons which are not effective?

Should they just sit back passively and take what is on offer?

Before judging and attributing blame for the underachievement of able pupils, have you listened to the voices of the pupils themselves and considered the context to which these comments apply?

---

explaining and who offer encouragement and high expectations in the classroom. These suggestions are developed under the headings of teacher–pupil consultation and teaching talk.

Teacher–pupil consultation

The authors also wish to emphasise that it pays to listen to the voices of Able Underachievers describing their own experiences if we seriously desire to facilitate achievement. Other researchers concur with the view that an important factor in the study of underachievement is the individual's perception and explanation of events (Dweck 1975, Bandura and Schunk 1981, Alderman 1990 and Leyden and Bennett 1995). Leyden and Bennett state that 'an exploration of the pupils' experience in their own school and their perceptions of what helps and hinders their own willingness and ability to achieve their best has to be the starting point.'

However, in highlighting this, the authors would want to stress that the processes involved in consultation should be reciprocal and involve a no-blame culture. The pupil may feel that the adult is critical: the adult may feel that the pupil is not prepared to demonstrate effort. Either way, this type of conversation is likely to further perpetuate the underachievement.

Facilitative conversations with Able Underachievers may be more productive if they occur out of the classroom. For some pupils, the best approach may be group consultation, in which the pupils' underachievement is considered in a problem-solving manner with the pupils themselves involved in discussion, not only with the teacher but also with a parent, sibling or peer of their choosing. Assuming that you, the reader, are an adult and that you would like to find a way of having a facilitative conversation with an Able Underachiever, you might simply start by asking yourself the following preliminary questions:

- What is the conversation that I have not yet had with this young person?
- What am I avoiding?
- What am I afraid of hearing?
- Why hasn't this conversation occurred spontaneously?
- Where should it take place?
- Should I initiate it or wait for someone else to do it?
- Should I invite the pupil to bring along others?
- Will it be a one-off conversation or the start of something regular?
- What could I say that I have not said before?
- What types of questions should I ask?
- What can I learn about others and myself from listening to this person?
- What needs to change and can I work with this person to facilitate this?

The aim of the conversation should be to give all participants an opportunity to share their own views and feel valued and respected for doing so. Possibilities for improving the situation should be encouraged by all. It might help to start with establishing some ground rules.

Teachers can help facilitate the discussion by the types of questions they ask. Many useful 'stock questions' can be taken from those used in Solution Focused Brief Therapy, examples of which are given in Figure 2.2 below. The effectiveness of this type of questioning is that it avoids focusing on the problem, analysing 'why' there is a problem or making judgements, but instead encourages the use of creative thinking (or what will be referred to in Chapter 4 as 'synthesis') by looking ahead to new possibilities.

In the authors' study, the pupils referred very little to meaningful interactions with adults, or to being invited to answer interesting questions, or to their personal views and opinions being heard. Much of the time they presented a picture of being either verbally passive or argumentative with adults. Analysis of pupil responses suggests that what is happening in these interactions is a lack of reciprocity and a potential misuse of power on the part of the adult to instil compliance. The need to find ways of improving communication and relationships between teacher and pupil is, therefore, highlighted. Some teachers would argue that there is little time or space for this type of consultation in school. Yet evidence from other research suggests this is a crucial factor relating to a student's willingness to engage in learning. Lee-Corbin and Denicolo (1998) state that 'one of the attributes of good teaching most commonly adduced by children was that a teacher should take a personal interest in each pupil.'

Teaching talk

Whether or not teachers find the time to 'consult' with underachieving pupils in the ways suggested above, there is strong evidence to suggest that the way teachers

How will you know if this discussion has been worthwhile?

What is happening in lessons when you are most interested and giving of your best?

Suppose you were starting this year again, what features would you like to be different?

What is your vision for your preferred future?

What needs to happen to help you get there?

What could be done to help you get there?

Who would be the best person to keep you on track, coach and monitor you?

How will you know if things are improving?

Figure 2.2 Examples of solution focused questioning

use talk in the classroom can be influential in raising motivation and achievement.

Significant in the authors' study was the Able Underachievers' strong view of the general rapport between the teacher and the class that can so often be enhanced by the use of humour. Lee-Corbin and Denicolo (1998) in their study of Able Achievers and Able Underachievers in primary schools also recognised the importance of humour in the classroom, describing how 'one teacher arranged a weekly joke telling session at the beginning of the story period, the last session of the day. This lasted for approximately five minutes and was very popular with all the children.'

The primary teachers in their study also felt strongly that if achievement was to occur, there needed to be a good rapport between pupil and teacher and a partnership between the teacher and parents. The pupils themselves when questioned felt that, to assist them to achieve, teachers needed to be helpful, have a sense of humour, take a personal interest in them, treat all pupils equally, be enthusiastic and kind but not overly strict. As observers of much classroom teaching over the years, the authors recognise that some teachers naturally possess the ability to use wit to engage pupils. There are many different ways of developing rapport in the classroom and most teachers will have their own style and skills, whether involving the use of humour or not. However, the Able Underachievers placed great value on the use of humour.

Teachers who do not find it easy to use verbal humour might consider using other media. For example, they might occasionally use amusing pictures, posters, quotes or riddles relating to the subject matter being taught to stimulate discussion, to challenge thinking or to capture attention. A further suggestion would be to set the class the challenge of bringing something relevant but humorous to the lesson.

Having considered ways of developing rapport, we turn next to considering the use of instructional language when teaching.

Locke and Beech (1991: 9) proposed twelve areas in their 'Profile of Language Use – Junior' to describe the expected language skills of children at Key Stage 2. Two of these areas are those of:

- Explaining – child explains activities, events, his or her own actions clearly and concisely.
- Instructing – child is able to give a sequence of instructions to an adult or peer to play a game, draw a specific picture, build a particular model from Lego, draw a route on a map, or a shape/object on squared paper following compass directions.

If this is true of pupils by the age of 11, then it surely must be true of adults. Kyriacou (1991) reminds us that it is the quality of teachers' talk that is one of the most important aspects of effective teaching. However, claims have also been made that many teacher explanations and instructions simply do not make sense (Allwright 1986).

> There is a wealth of research evidence to support the claim that clarity of explanation makes a major contribution to greater educational attainment . . . explanations should by and large try to be grammatically simple, explicit, make good use of examples, define any technical terms, and, most importantly, not go on for too long! (Kyriacou 1991: 35, 37)

Yet Able Underachievers, despite their ability, can be confused by the subject content and experience the frustration of being taught by some teachers who do not explain well, lack focus and ramble. Teachers who want to focus on their skills in this area could begin by reflecting on their skills in explaining or instructing. Brown and Hatton (1982) in their book *Explanations and Explaining* provide an observation schedule (Table 2.1) for a colleague to use in assessing 'explaining' skills. Alternatively, the use of such a schedule could be enhanced through audio-taping or better still, video feedback.

A teacher may glean ideas from the observation schedule in the table for enhancing skills of explanation, but may feel that the exercise in itself is too impractical or involved. Perhaps a more useful summary of points to note can be gained from the developments of a later work of Brown and Armstrong (1984) as seen in Figure 2.3.

Having considered good practice in the use of instructional language, we turn next to the importance attached to the types of questions used in teaching. We might consider an answer to the question 'Is meaningful dialogue taking place within classrooms?' Wheldall and Glynn (1989) state that 'conversation qualifies as

Table 2.1 Observation schedule for explaining (Brown and Hatton 1982: 35)

Tick under the most appropriate heading	Always = A Usually = U Sometimes = S Once = O Never = N					
Skill observed	**A**	**U**	**S**	**O**	**N**	**Comments**
Clear introduction						
New terms clarified						
Apt word choice						
Clear sentence structure						
Vagueness avoided						
Adequate concrete examples						
Within pupil's experience						
Voice used to emphasise						
Emphasis by gesture						
Appropriate pauses						
Direct verbal cueing						
Repetition used						
Main ideas paraphrased						
Sound use of media/materials						
Pattern of explanation clear						
Parts linked to each other						
Progressive summary						
Pace or level altered						
Opportunity for pupil questions						
Grasp of main ideas checked						
Pupil commitment sought						

a responsive social context; merely responding to adult questions and instructions does not.'

With reference to 'teacher talk' Tough (1979) notes the difficulty for teachers in organising their teaching so that meaningful dialogue plays a major part. However, she points out that it is the way that teachers modify their use of language that is crucial in order to develop effective forms of communication with students and promote understanding. Morgan and Saxton (1991) also stress that teachers need

> Clarity and fluency: through defining new terms clearly and appropriate use of explicit language
>
> Emphasis and interest: making good use of voice, gestures, materials and paraphrasing
>
> Using examples: appropriate in type and quality
>
> Organisation: presence of a logical sequence and use of link words and phrases
>
> Feedback: offering a chance for pupils to ask questions and assessing learning outcomes

Figure 2.3 Aide-mémoire – five basic skills in effective explaining (Brown and Armstrong 1984)

to be able to ask different types of questions to generate different types of learning. Another researcher in this field, Kerry, in the 1980s, found that teachers tend to use a predominance of question forms relating to lower levels of thinking, for example seeking to find out how much pupils know and understand. What is needed to engage able pupils is the inclusion of question forms that elicit higher order thinking. Kerry (1983) defines questioning as 'ferreting about in the mind of another person to explore his or her depth and range of response.'

However, this is only part of the picture and we are reminded of Flanders' (1970) two-thirds rule noting the predominance of teacher talk in classrooms, and the point made earlier of the need for greater reciprocity in dialogue between teacher and student. In the guidance manual for teachers, *Able Pupils – Providing for Able Pupils and Those with Exceptional Talent* (Nottinghamshire County Council, September 2000), reference is made to the need for able children to be provided with opportunities to develop *their own* questions in classrooms where a culture of enquiry is encouraged.

Robert Fisher, Head of the Centre for Thinking Skills at Brunel University, in his many talks to teachers often refers to the usefulness of 'think books', where children are encouraged to record comments or questions of interest to them. With older able pupils the term 'problem posing' is used as a reminder to teachers that young people need to be encouraged to generate problems to solve rather than always solving the problems posed by others. The concept of 'think books' can translate into 'think logs' at secondary level and be used for a variety of purposes beyond problem posing, such as pupil self-evaluation of learning and thinking styles.

Referring again to the 'Profile of Language Use – Junior' (Locke and Beech 1991:9), we can select another two areas of competence expected of children by the age of 11:

- Extended Use of Questions – child can contribute to discussion to devise a set of questions to pursue a line of enquiry.
- Inferring and Deducing – child's questions, answers, comments and explanations and so on show evidence of deduction and inference.

The authors, with reference to the secondary aged pupils who contributed to their study, would argue that by the age of 13 or so, many able pupils will have suppressed their desire to question out loud or contribute to discussion, which perhaps they had previously enjoyed in primary school. The shift in teaching at Key Stage 3 is characterised by a need to commit much thought and debate to written forms of communication and (we can speculate) pressure by teachers to deliver quantity of curriculum content at the expense of quality of thought. Morgan and Saxton (1991) believe that 'we limit the power of learning if we regard teachers solely as transmitters and students solely as receivers in classroom interaction.'

It is worth mentioning at this point the work of Brown and Wragg (1993) who explore the use of effective questioning in classrooms. They point out that not only do we need to consider the types of questions that we ask (for example, narrow questions that elicit recall and broad, thought-provoking questions), but also the tactics of asking these questions. Effective questioning involves:

- structuring;
- pitching and putting clearly;
- directing and distributing;
- pausing and pacing;
- prompting and probing;
- listening and responding; and
- sequencing.

(Brown and Wragg 1993)

This model encompasses a number of the points already made. However, knowing the above does not necessarily imply that adults are skilled in questioning this way. What Brown and Wragg propose is that adults can develop effective forms of questioning by minimising errors. They highlight some of the common errors in questioning that, if couched in positive terms, could be developed into an observational schedule similar to the one described earlier for giving explanations. See Table 2.2.

If this analysis seems impractical or too detailed, a simpler version would be to reflect on the following 'sample investigative questions' adapted from those suggested by Nunan (1989: 35). Some teachers have used the following checklist to reflect usefully on a taped transcript of a sample of lessons taught:

- How much talking do I do? Is this too little or too much?
- What happens when I vary the amount of talking I do?

Table 2.2 Observation schedule for effective questioning (adapted with permission from Brown and Wragg 1993: 18)

Tick under the most appropriate heading	Always = A Usually = U Sometimes = S Once = O Never = N					
Skill observed	**A**	**U**	**S**	**O**	**N**	**Comments**
Asking only one question at a time						
Asking a question and allowing others to answer it						
Asking questions of pupils other than those able/likeable						
Asking a difficult question once in the discussion						
Asking relevant questions						
Asking different types of questions						
Asking questions in a non-threatening manner						
Indicating a change in the type of question being asked						
Using probing questions						
Giving the young person time to think						
Correcting wrong answers						
Listening to and valuing all answers						
Building on answers						

- Do I give the other person time to respond ?
- What type of questions do I ask? Are they 'display' or 'referential'? (See below.)
- What typical patterns of interaction are there between myself and the young person?

Nunan (1989) makes the distinction between 'display questions' (ones to which the questioner knows the answer) and 'referential questions' (ones to which the person asking the question does not know the answer). He found that display questions characterise classroom interaction almost to the exclusion of referential questions, which tend to be used outside the classroom. What we might conclude from this is that if adults invest more time asking questions of Able Underachievers of the 'referential type' both inside and outside the classroom, this could facilitate conversation and achievement.

There are many questions that could be asked, but it could be suggested that there is a tendency for the type of questions asked of Able Underachievers to be presented in a way that sounds judgemental, implies criticism and is centred around perceived weaknesses of lack of motivation, poor grades and unfinished assignments. If we consider for a moment the needs of able pupils, this can provide some starting points for the questions used in facilitative conversations. Sadler (2000a) drawing conclusions from her work with Able Underachievers and adapting ideas previously presented by Barry Teare (1997), summarises these as follows:

- high teacher expectations;
- recognition and celebration of abilities and achievements;
- encouragement to take risks with opportunities to fail;
- thinking time and places to 'park' thoughts;
- a classroom of enquiry;
- opportunity to work at an increased pace;
- opportunities to collaborate with age peers and like minds;
- recognition of all needs including social skills/play;
- recording skills and self-esteem;
- recognition of and support in weak areas;
- a challenging curriculum, promoting higher order thinking skills through differentiated tasks and questioning;
- recognition of prior knowledge;
- encouragement to formulate questions and pose problems;
- more independence of study and promotion of study skills;
- access to resources (e.g. libraries and information technology);
- ability to recognise and self-reflect on process skills;
- creative teaching and learning opportunities;
- recognition and advancement of specific talents;
- time to explore areas of interest in depth; and
- extra-curricular opportunities.

The types of referential questions asked by teachers and parents can, therefore, be linked to the particular needs of Able Underachievers:

- questions to elicit prior knowledge and encourage pupil questioning;
- questions to raise expectations;
- questions to stimulate higher order thinking of the topic being taught;
- questions to encourage creativity and risk taking;
- questions that acknowledge and develop weak areas;
- questions that clarify pupil needs and aim to reduce underachievement; and
- questions to encourage self-reflection.

One of the main strands of the *Key Stage 3 National Pilot on Teaching and Learning in the Foundation Subjects* (DfES 2001) involves the teaching of thinking skills. To achieve this involves effective teaching through the use of questioning and providing clear explanations.

To elaborate on these areas, consider the examples of 'scripts' in Table 2.3 that can be used by adults in their attempts to have facilitative conversations.

Clearly there is an overlap in the suggested 'referential questions' between what could usefully be employed by teachers in teacher–pupil consultation and also with reference to teaching talk.

Before we leave this chapter on 'communication' let us return to our knowledge of language use. Earlier in this chapter, reference was made to the skills of language use that children normally develop by the age of 11. Writers such as Crystal (1987) and Locke and Beech (1991) who have devoted most of their energy to the study of language would be quick to highlight the fact that language continues to develop

Table 2.3 An aide-mémoire for using referential questions in conversations with Able Underachievers

Question type	Examples
To elicit prior knowledge and enquiry	What do you know about this subject already? What do you want to find out? What have you learnt?
To raise expectations	This is what I expect: how can you make it even better?
To stimulate higher order thinking	What are the advantages and disadvantages of? (analysis) What would the world be like if? (synthesis) What is your opinion about? (evaluation)
To encourage creativity	Can you change this to make something else? How could you do this a different way? How could you present this without using words?
To develop weak areas	How long can you work at . . . ? What's stopping you from getting ahead? What targets would you set to improve?
To clarify pupil needs	How do you learn best? What really interests you? Do you ever feel frustrated in class? Why? What would you change about your class or school?
To encourage self-reflection	Did you share your ideas with others? Did you start by making a plan? Did you explain the way you worked?

well into the school years and beyond. Locke and Beech developed 'Profiles of Language Use' for pre-school, infant and junior aged children, but did not explore beyond this. See Table 2.4.

The authors would like to propose a model of 'Language Use for Adults' to encapsulate many of the points highlighted in this chapter which relate to the language used by adults in social and academic contexts. The reader may wish to compare the language use of junior aged children with the proposed language use of adults and contemplate the gulf that exists in linguistic competence between the age of 11 years and adulthood (see model below.) An interesting exercise would be to estimate how many adults you know who are effective communicators. Next time you listen to a TV show like *Coronation Street* or *EastEnders*, notice the patterns of speech that you hear from different characters who tend to repeat verbal scripts and phrases. It is easy to lapse into an overuse of types of language that can be barriers to communicating effectively with others. By adolescence, most able pupils have acquired competence in the use of language expected of pupils of junior age. However, to acquire adult structures of language use can take many years, even for able adults in professional positions. Consider the 'Profile of Language Use' for adults outlined in Table 2.4 when answering the questions below.

Questions for the reader

Can you identify your own strengths and weaknesses within the profile of adult language use?

What ideas could you take from this chapter to help you develop your skills in communicating further?

If you are to have facilitative conversations with an Able Underachiever, which types of language use do you feel you need to be most aware of promoting in your conversations?

Summary

For teachers who are looking to develop their skills in communicating with Able Underachievers the following key points represent opportunities for change:

- Begin to repair communications with Able Underachievers by asking yourself some preliminary questions that may then lead to facilitative conversations.
- Find opportunities to consult with Able Underachievers and take a personal interest in them, preferably out of the classroom. Avoid making judgements,

Table 2.4 Profiles of Language Use

Profile of language use – Junior (Locke and Beech 1991: 9)	Profile of language use – Adult (Pomerantz, K.A. 2000)
Initiation of conversation with unfamiliar adults and children – Child has the confidence to initiate conversations with unfamiliar people by commenting, volunteering information or asking questions.	**Social exchange** –Adult can initiate conversations with familiar and unfamiliar others to indicate concern, care, express interest and show respect.
Projection of thoughts and feelings – Child can consider and describe the thoughts and feelings that might be felt by self and others in a range of situations, familiar and less familiar.	**Reciprocity** – Adult shows the ability to listen to and appreciate the thoughts and views of others and can describe their own feelings in return.
Instructing – Child is able to give a sequence of instructions to an adult or peer to play a game, draw a specific picture, build a particular model from Lego, draw a route on a map, or shape/object on squared paper following compass directions.	**Instructing** – Adult is able to give a sequence of instructions to another adult or a child to enable them to complete a task.
Explaining – Child explains activities, events, his or her own actions clearly and concisely.	**Explaining** – Adult is able to explain in a manner that is focused, clear and concise.
Imaginative use of language – Child uses a wide range of vocabulary to express imaginative thinking in talking, drama, puppetry, writing and so on.	**Prosody** – Adult can deliberately modify aspects of voice and intonation to add emphasis to their use of vocabulary to express their thoughts (the ability to use gesture would be an added feature).
Extended use of questions – Child can contribute to discussion to devise a set of questions to pursue a line of enquiry.	**Questioning** – Adult can use a variety of question types (display and referential) to stimulate thinking and elicit the opinions of others.

Planning – Child is able to think ahead to decide equipment and steps required to complete a task; can describe to others.

Hypothesising – Child is able to suggest possible explanations of events.

Inferring and deducing – Child's questions, answers, comments, explanations and so on show evidence of deduction and inference.

Reflecting on and exploring language – Child shows an interest in language, by recognising and appreciating puns, understanding and making simple jokes, participating in activities for extending vocabulary and so on.

Presenting sequenced oral account – Child can deliver an oral story or account of events in clear and concise chronological order.

Giving and considering opinions – Child will give a reasoned opinion on a range of experiences, activities and issues. He or she will consider alternative opinions and discuss them.

Planning – Adult can think ahead to decide equipment and steps required to complete a task; can discuss, compare and modify with others.

Hypothesising – Adult can present various theories relating to phenomena and events based on reasoned explanation and deduction.

Debating – Adult can present a reasoned argument giving credence to one view that contrasts with another.

Manipulating – Adults can play with words to twist and elaborate meanings to evoke humour in others. They can also invent new vocabulary and colloquialisms.

Presenting – Adult can present a logical account of events to inspire or entertain others such as a key note speech or in story telling.

Conflict resolution – Adult will consider the position of someone whose views are contradictory to theirs, will seek out the common ground and propose a compromise.

Adapted from the *Teaching Procedures Handbook: Teaching Talking* © A. Locke and M. Beech 1991, by permission of the Authors and the Publishers, nferNelson Publishing Company Limited.

implying criticism or focusing on perceived weaknesses of low motivation, poor grades, poorly presented work and unfinished assignments. Alternatively use 'referential' and solution-focused questions to elicit possibilities for change.

- Remember that Able Underachievers like teachers who explain clearly, listen, show social respect, are humorous, friendly and positive, ask open questions and have high expectations. Make use of observational tools and aide-mémoires to reflect on 'teaching talk' in classrooms.
- Ask different types of questions to stimulate different types of thinking and learning. Encourage students to generate their own questions in classrooms where a culture of enquiry is fostered.
- Consider your own skills of language use when reflecting on how well you communicate with Able Underachievers and what you can do to develop these skills. Not all adults are effective communicators and the skills of developing the social use of language extend well into adulthood.

Suggestions for further reading

Ajmal, Y. and Rees, I. (eds) (2001) *Solutions in Schools: Creative applications of solution focused brief thinking with young people and adults.* London: BT Press.

Morgan, N. and Saxton, J. (1991) *Teaching, Questioning and Learning.* London: Routledge.

Wheldall, K. and Glynn, T. (1989) *Effective Classroom Learning.* Oxford: Blackwell.

CHAPTER 3

Developing relationships with peers, siblings and parents

The next theme highlighted by the Able Underachievers relates to relationships they have with their peers, siblings and parents and how this influences their learning.

- Able Underachievers perceive some conflict between meeting competing needs from teachers' and friends' expectations but tend to try to strike a compromise. They do not seem to grasp fully the nature of the conflict but tend to address it as a simple problem that requires a simple compromise solution.
- They really value friendships but seem to have little contact with or understanding of Able Achievers and reject the social costs of being called a 'square', 'swot', 'nerd', 'spoff' or 'geek'. The peer group culture exerts considerable pressure on Able Underachievers. Able Underachievers fear that hard work and self-discipline might disadvantage their social life and make them boring.
- These students have clear and worrying views about the social costs of becoming an Able Achiever but lack much opportunity to get to know Able Achievers well and delve beneath the stereotypes. This is another lost opportunity.
- These pupils do not appear to access much regular peer support and encouragement for academic work as they might do if they played for a team. The peer culture does little to encourage achievement. Able Underachievers believe their friends think more or less as they do about these issues.
- These young people might work harder if teachers were more encouraging and nurtured a more relaxed, interactive and sociable classroom environment. Able Underachievers seem to take little responsibility for this. Perhaps they do not feel teachers are interested in their suggestions.
- Able Underachievers can get valued help from siblings but the scope of this seems limited and underdeveloped. They respect able older siblings but this respect and acceptance of support does not extend to improving their relationships with Able Achievers in school.
- They mostly use parents in a limited homework surveillance role with mixed results. This is another lost opportunity for sharing a much wider range of facilitative and stimulating communication and activities with their parents which sadly only a minority seem to access.

Figure 3.1 Key research outcomes specific to the theme of the relationships that Able Underachievers have with their peers, siblings and parents

What the pupils said about conflicts of interests between teachers and friends

Q15. How often do you feel there is a conflict of interest between advice from your teachers and your friends?

This question was intended was to estimate the scope of conflicts in which Able Underachievers felt torn between following their friends and obeying the instructions of teachers. While six admitted that this conflict happens 'often' 16 (equating to 62 per cent of those interviewed) tended to minimise it or deny that it was a problem. Some acknowledged a plan to conform with the wishes of staff. A larger number sought workable compromises such as trying to satisfy school demands like getting homework done on time while accepting invitations to go out with friends who perhaps were less worried about meeting deadlines and completing assigned tasks.

Interpretation

This question might have given us greater insight into why Able Underachievers actually underachieve by showing us the bind that some Able Underachievers face on a regular basis. However, the majority of our respondents did not really see it that way. Perhaps some did not fully appreciate the meaning of the term 'conflict of interest'. When a pupil looked confused on this question it was modified to focus on the specific situation where friends wanted the Able Underachiever to go out, but the homework was not yet done, as an example. The Able Underachievers seemed skilled at finding ways to compromise so perhaps that means that they did not really perceive a genuine lasting conflict. The potential for conflict had been anticipated and overcome to their satisfaction.

It would have been interesting to see if the teachers agreed with this self-analysis that the work for school was getting sufficient attention and was completed to a reasonable academic standard. As cited earlier, many parents of Able Under-achievers felt it was necessary to keep a close surveillance on the completion of homework rather than leaving it to the discretion of the Able Underachiever.

The 'cat and mouse' game used to be played with enthusiasm in workplaces such as factories, until managers and workers both discovered that it was self-defeating and that no one was winning. Is it not time we realised that this kind of game which is influenced by the relationships between teachers, pupils and parents can be a 'no win' situation that continually perpetuates underachievement?

> **Questions for the reader**
>
> If you walked into this conflict yourself, what might you say to either of the parties involved?
>
> What would you expect them to say in reply?

Q30. Imagine that your teachers want you to do A. Your friends want you to do B instead. Think of an example. What do you usually do?

The question was designed to provide an insight into the often competing influences of teachers and friends. It was assumed that Able Underachievers frequently expended less effort than Able Achievers, and that Able Underachievers found excuses to engage in activities focusing on peers rather than always addressing academic curriculum demands as a priority. The authors wanted to know how independent the Able Underachievers could be in the face of temptation to follow the crowd or their peers rather than meet reasonable expectations for the completion of tasks set by teachers.

Most Able Underachievers were able to think of an example. For those who could not, once again the scenario offered was the conflict in which the student is torn between satisfying the homework requirements of the teacher and invitations from friends to go out in the evening instead. Only two (8 per cent) were uncertain. The vast majority were inclined either to conform with the homework demands, or else find a creative compromise that allowed both conditions to be met. An example of this might be rushing home to get homework, or some of it, done quickly, thus allowing sufficient time to still accompany friends going out, even if it meant working later in the evening in order to complete homework. Four Able Underachievers (15 per cent) said that, in conflicts, they would be more inclined to follow the influence of friends. Two were clear that they could make an independent situation-specific decision without being unduly influenced by either teachers or friends.

Interpretation

It is encouraging once again (as with Question 15) to see that Able Underachievers perceive themselves to be generally capable of assessing a conflict situation and then taking appropriate action which usually works to their satisfaction. There is no clear data here to suggest that the Able Underachievers are unreasonably influenced by the social crowd leading them astray, if we are to believe their own interpretation of potentially conflicting situations. What the authors' findings do seem to clarify further is that these Able Underachievers appear to have a well-developed repertoire of social skills.

> ### Questions for the reader
>
> Once again the Able Underachievers do not really see a conflict here which interferes with their lives in a big way. What is your reaction to this?
>
> They seem to indicate that they can handle it or manage it. Is this convincing?

What the pupils said about clever pupils in school

Q14. In this school what do your friends think about clever pupils?

As already noted, clever pupils are conspicuous in school, and value judgements are made about them by others from an early age. What one feels about oneself is often influenced by the competence and capability of others at school. Reactions vary from admiration to contempt, from respect to derision and from cooperation to jealousy. This question sought to establish just how Able Underachievers perceived how these clever pupils were accepted or rejected by the peer group in schools.

This question tended to produce longer responses characterised by some confusion about terminology, with particular reference to negative or pejorative terms like 'squares', 'geeks', 'spoffs', 'swots' and 'nerds'. While some Able Underachievers were prepared to offer a crude definition of what these words meant or might mean, most said that one or two terms were used in their schools, but tended to deny using the words themselves. They acknowledged the general confusion about what these words meant.

Sometimes these unfortunate social labels were associated with the notion of being a 'teachers' pet'. Most agreed that the terms carried a negative connotation and that they would not want the terms to be applied to themselves. In general, the Able Underachievers acknowledged being above average in intelligence but would not always call themselves 'clever'. The confusion arose when these words were used inconsistently. The clever pupils were seen as popular with teachers, probably due to their self-discipline, high academic output and accomplishments and their conformity, while perhaps being less popular with other pupils. Some Able Achievers were, admittedly, well liked.

For many, the connotations of holding any of these labels meant a life that was more solitary, perhaps boring, and open to teasing and taunting. Occasionally, this bad treatment was partially justified by the alleged practice of some able pupils (Able Achievers) showing contempt for the less able, but more often the Able Underachievers wanted to defend those they saw as innocent and getting a bad deal at school. They certainly did not want to join the ostracised able pupils and suffer social exclusion. At times, Able Underachievers showed great compassion for those negatively labelled by the peer group.

Able Underachievers offered some interventions to stop the maltreatment of able pupils when it became excessive. They drew comparisons with anti-bullying strategies that can be effective in any situation involving teasing either in or out of school. They suggested that schools set higher standards to raise the attainments of those doing the teasing of Able Achievers, offered advice to those teasing, intervened with sanctions as necessary, encouraged Able Achievers to stop showing off or being condescending and used surveillance appropriately to identify norm violators who made life difficult for others at school.

Interpretation

It has been suggested that schools do more to celebrate success conspicuously among the able pupil population. The Able Underachievers do not see much payoff for changing their life style, which honours the need and value of having a social life and of not being a social bore or stigmatised. Gross (1994) terms this the 'forced choice dilemma', where for some pupils a strong psychosocial need is sought at the expense of individual intellectual fulfilment. The Able Underachievers studied identify the existence of peer influence in terms of preferred social identity but appear to deny that this contributes to an avoidance of work demands. Able Underachievers would need some powerful convincing that they are really missing out on great opportunities to be inspired and challenged to greater accomplishments and all the fulfilment and satisfaction that could come from using the talents they possess and attaining higher standards.

At present, Able Underachievers simply do not see how a radical or modest change in lifestyle could be accomplished without great cost socially and in terms of hard work. Anyone who has grown accustomed to using less energy than required for a long time develops a habit that others might label as 'lazy' or 'idle'. Perhaps if they had better and regular access to Able Achiever role models who are doing well socially, are not viciously attacked by prejudice and who have a full and balanced social life in and outside of school, this might help.

Questions for the reader

How might Able Underachievers gain better access to these Able Achiever role models?

Who might organise this or facilitate it happening as it is unlikely to happen spontaneously?

If teachers of late have seen prejudices based on ethnicity or bullying successfully confronted with a more inclusive philosophy, is it not possible for them to challenge the language that describes some of the student population as 'squares', 'geeks', 'spoffs', 'swots' and 'nerds?'

What might be an appropriate response from either a teacher or an Able Underachiever when terms like these are used openly in school?

Could we start by asking those using the terms (and those listening) to tell us what they mean and the intent behind their public use in school?

The possibility of achieving at a higher level and having a positive self-image and a bit of popularity as well sounds like a package that might need some selling, at least to a number of the Able Underachievers interviewed.

What the pupils said about pupils whose company they value

Q10. Tell me about the other pupils that you like to spend time with. What are they like?

This question was used to build up a picture of the type of friends with whom Able Underachievers choose to spend their social time. The trend seemed to be that Able Underachievers value friends who are:

- socially skilful
- talkative
- friendly

- humorous
- supportive
- trustworthy

- fun to be with
- relaxed
- share similar interests

A few generated the impression that they tended to associate with other clever pupils, but the majority seemed to value diversity among friends and were not seeking a subgroup of exclusively hard-working and self-disciplined associates.

Some went so far as to describe the different social groups, highlighting the gap between the popular students and those who they perceive as socially disadvantaged but clever pupils described as 'squares', 'geeks', 'spoffs', 'swots' and 'nerds'. Only one out of the cohort proffer the view that the latter labels might apply to him. The rest implied that there were serious social costs to being so labelled and that they would prefer to occupy something of a 'middle of the road' or less conspicuous position. Perhaps Able Underachievers distance themselves from pupils with these labels and feel that they apply more accurately to Able Achievers who work harder, get better grades, are more popular with teachers, etc. but may unfortunately suffer some ostracism from other pupils.

Interpretation

For those teachers who are hoping to save or rescue some Able Underachievers from a self-defeating career in school, there is a major obstacle that must be addressed. Able Underachievers are perceptive and quick to spot all the inherent social disadvantages and costs that they might have to pay (conspicuously) if they are to change their lifestyles and work harder. Several respondents said that the socially disadvantaged pupils ought to 'get a life'. Able Underachievers see a relationship between this neglect of addressing one's social needs and the high probability of becoming a bore.

Enabling Able Underachievers to re-examine this thinking would be no small task. If Able Underachievers were given greater opportunity to engage in exciting extra-curricular activities with better, Able Achieving role models who were not stereotyped as 'squares', 'geeks', 'spoffs', 'swots' and 'nerds' this might widen their horizons and challenge prejudiced thinking. An example might be an Able Underachiever interested in music but not doing much with it at school. Spending a summer playing in a band or working in a recording studio might precipitate a renewed interest in exploring more thoroughly what was possible with music back in school in September.

Questions for the reader

Can readers sense the real gulf between where Able Underachievers feel they are safely located now and where they fear they might be isolated socially if they really started to work conspicuously much harder in school and with homework?

Can readers make suggestions as to how to sell the message that acquiring a negative stigma or label is not inevitable, incurable or lethal?

Is it possible to be a popular Able Achiever? How can we encourage Able Underachievers to believe this?

What the pupils said about other pupils influencing Able Underachievers

Q11. What do other pupils do to encourage or discourage your progress in school?

This question was intended to examine the influence of the Able Underachievers' peer group as another factor that applies both within and outside of school. Able Underachievers did identify certain actions by peers that facilitate their progress with work at school. This includes:

- encouragement
- praise
- inspiration
- help
- working together (group work)
- constructive criticism
- giving clues or suggestions
- explaining
- setting a good example
- giving advice

On the negative side Able Underachievers identified the following actions by their peers that interfere with learning and hinder progress:

- distracting
- disrupting
- talking inappropriately
- discouraging
- teasing
- damaging work
- annoying people

Many of these observations seemed to be anecdotal and about spontaneous incidents rather than planned and regular occurrences. There did not seem to be much in terms of organised procedures that would help Able Underachievers access much needed peer support to do better at school. It is possible that Able Achievers access more of this support but, if so, it was not mentioned as something observed by Able Underachievers in school settings.

Interpretation

There is no doubt that pupils are influenced positively and negatively by their peers. In secondary education, the peer group gains influence while parents seem to lose some influence. In competitive team sports there is a contagious effect through which peer influence can stimulate a team into winning. Athletes on television frequently give testimony to how much enthusiasm and energy they gain from loyal fans yelling messages of support from the stands.

The boost that can come from encouragement, attention and praise is well documented. With the Able Underachievers in this cohort the interviews found little such positive academic influence of friends on a regular basis. Many Able Underachievers did acknowledge help and occasional assistance from friends but there were no comments about a 'hothouse effect' where personal effort was buoyed up by regular sustained camaraderie and support to achieve new and higher standards and complete projects. No one among the Able Underachievers mentioned feeling really valued or supported for a performance of any type at school. Perhaps they felt they had done little to deserve it. Perhaps if such peer support were available they would not show much interest in receiving it.

Optimists might feel that Able Underachievers really do not need the positive influence from peers to work harder at school. Realists would argue that Able Underachievers need support wherever they can find it because of entrenched patterns of under-functioning that began earlier in life and are resistant to change.

Questions for the reader

If adolescence is a period of greater peer influence as the parents take a 'backseat', what could be done to enlist peer support?

Could adults strive to change the environment that does so little to value achievement amongst Able Underachievers?

If you could talk to the peer group (especially Able Achievers) about being more helpful and encouraging to Able Underachievers, what would you say to them?

What pupils said about the work environment

Q28. *What would make you work harder?*

Here we asked Able Underachievers for suggested incentives, school changes and further interventions that might raise the level of measured output when it came to school work. If one drew a comparison (figuratively speaking) for the sake of argument with track and field events within athletics, the Able Achievers appeared to be running and working up a sweat. The Able Underachievers were walking and rarely breaking into a sweat. This phenomenon is true of most schools and is obvious to the whole school community. Different groups, however, would have different views as to the causes of it.

Six (23 per cent) were clear that they did not have a contribution to make here. The others offered a good cross-section of proposals. Many thought that incentives, rewards, praise, commendation, encouragement and extra privileges would make a big difference. Some wanted to change the classroom environment by making it less noisy, more interesting, better organised, more fun, less intrusive and more sociable and by providing more variety and choice. Some felt that the selective addition of music might be helpful. One stressed the value of goals, challenges, targets and deadlines. One thought that punishment would help. Some felt they would work harder if separated into sets, thereby reducing the influence of some peers. Some stressed the value of the teacher being firm. Some had unique contributions which are reproduced below:

Subject 8: Err I suppose if like the class was like more relaxed and the teachers weren't so strict it would help . . . if the teachers would always let you just like chat a bit but make sure you get on with your work still.

Subject 16: . . . like [teachers] talk to you and take an interest.
Subject 18: . . . if someone's like always encouraging you but like not always standing over you . . .

Subject 3: If you can achieve something at the end of it.

Subject 5: Probably if there was something I wanted to aim for and I knew I'd got to get a certain grade for it then I'd set a target and go for it.

Subject 7: . . . in a good environment where I'd feel like sort of part of it and erm . . . sort of people are like know each other and they can talk to each other and like not loads of noise but sort of talking and the teacher just goes round saying 'Are you all right?' and sort of like when you need to talk to them and stuff. . . just a relaxed environment really.

Interpretation

Able Underachievers seem well aware of just what might motivate them to work harder at school. They have ideas, but most of them seem to rely on an external locus of control. This means they attribute causation to some source outside of themselves. We did not hear these pupils talking confidently about their long-term plans to improve the school setting with their own suggestions. It was more detached in that they would come up with proposals that really required action and effort mostly by the teaching staff rather than involving activity that was within the control of the Able Underachievers. This continued to sound like the problem was owned by the teachers rather than the Able Underachievers

At this stage readers are invited to take a position on exactly what might make Able Underachievers work harder. The Able Underachievers responded to Question 28 with a tendency to focus on what others could or should do to make them inclined to try harder at school tasks. They were not placing great emphasis on what they themselves could be doing.

Questions for the reader

If you were asked for your views on what would make Able Underachievers work harder, would you feel that teachers should change their approach or would you be asking Able Underachievers to take responsibility to propose and then implement the necessary changes?

Are Able Underachievers more likely to commit to innovations they produce themselves, perhaps via an innovative school council?

If teachers were to do all the work here, the Able Underachievers might just passively sit back and do very little. Do you agree with this?

Where would you place your hopes of change?

Could either Able Underachievers or teachers launch this exercise without the suggestions coming from outside the school?

If they could, what has stopped this from happening spontaneously in schools already?

If you think it has happened already in some schools why have the Able Underachievers interviewed here made so little reference to successful interventions, regardless of who gets the credit for the success?

What the pupils said about the influence of siblings

Q13. Do your brothers or sisters exert any influence on your work and if so how?

This was an attempt to determine the amount of influence that a sibling could exert on school progress. About 80 per cent of students in school have a sibling (Smith *et al.* 1998: 111) so we would expect to lose a few respondents without siblings with this question. Prior to asking questions about parents and siblings, Able Underachievers were asked about family composition and when it became apparent that an only child was being interviewed this question was omitted.

About half the cohort felt that sibling influence was minimal or nil. In some cases their siblings were younger. Where the siblings were older (as applied in 12 cases), Able Underachievers gave generally positive ratings to siblings especially for:

- being helpful
- being encouraging
- serving as a good role model
- loaning materials
- offering explanations

Subject 19: . . . if I ever feel like I don't understand anything I just ask my older brother . . . cus he's a year above me.

Subject 5: . . .me sisters they both came to this school and me sister she did well in her maths so if I ever need any help in my maths she helps me and she'll help me in most subjects.

Those few who were critical of sibling influence mentioned interference and annoyance which can disturb learning and homework. These comments related to younger siblings.

Interpretation

We know that siblings (especially older siblings) can be a constructive influence with Able Underachievers, but it is expected that this is a resource that many Able Underachievers fail to fully access for a variety of reasons. In looking to draw up a list of potential allies who might be of help to Able Underachievers in reversing the pattern of underachievement, we ought not to forget what siblings might be able to offer if obstacles can be overcome. It is possible that older able siblings could do much to dispel the myths and stereotypes surrounding Able Achievers in school.

Questions for the reader

If you were placed in a position to meet with siblings of Able Underachievers what might you ask them?

Would you have any advice to offer them?

What the pupils said about parents influencing Able Underachievers

At this stage in the interview Able Underachievers were asked, 'Who do you live with at home?' Responses were used to individualise the following questions. In the text that follows 'parents' is used generically to mean 'parent(s)' or 'carer(s)'.

Q9. What do your parent(s) or [carer(s)] do to encourage or discourage your progress in school?

This question departs from the school-based environment and seeks to see just how effectively one out-of-school influence (namely parents) exerts a force on Able Underachievers in their school work. Again respondents had a choice as to whether to focus on positive or negative aspects of this particular influence. If the Able Underachiever responded only in one way then the other was addressed in a follow-up question.

   This question generally seemed to elicit responses that referred to the monitoring or checking role that parents take in supervising the completion of homework and the preparation for tests. It was cited far more frequently than any other type of parental influence (such as celebration) over student progress at school. The findings reported here suggested that some Able Underachievers actually valued this parental role and had grown accustomed to it and perhaps relied on it as a coping strategy. Another sizeable subgroup of Able Underachievers resented the lack of trust and wanted parents 'off my back' when it came to homework. Others reported this surveillance as a mixed blessing that held both advantages and costs to the parties involved.

Other positive parental acts included:

- offering advice
- being generally encouraging
- giving praise
- trusting
- supporting
- rewarding
- acknowledging
- instructing

- solving problems
- nudging
- reminding
- revising
- focusing
- signing reports
- setting standards

Able Underachievers were critical of other parental behaviours as not being helpful and actually hindering achievements and progress at school. This list consisted of:

- shouting (are Able Underachievers particularly sensitive to this phenomenon?);
- becoming overly involved, especially with outdated or obsolete homework strategies;
- nagging;
- demanding;
- moaning;
- being overly critical;
- not respecting the student's needs for autonomy and space;
- being overly pessimistic; and
- stating very low expectations of success in school assessments and tests.

What emerges here are a considerable number of parallel statements about the positive and negative characteristics of both teachers and parents that are significant in the eyes of Able Underachievers.

One student said that he would work more productively if his parents were less involved with checking up on his work. Yet he claims his parents have not been told this and that he would be likely to be punished for suggesting this strategy to them.

Interpretation

There is strong reason to believe that parents can exert a positive influence over exactly what is being done at home to prepare for school, provided that the pattern of communication between all parties is open, honest and constructive. There is no magic formula specifying how to structure parental support, but the voices of the Able Underachievers hint that often there is a subtle game taking place, involving all sorts of talk and action or inaction that can be both productive and damaging. When the communication is facilitative everyone gains.

Perhaps the solution is a more open and mutually agreed contract between the pupil and the parent that recognises the talents and gifts of the Able Underachiever in using his or her own diagnostic skills to establish the right balance between gentle support and surveillance. It needs an evaluation feedback loop, allowing all parties to renegotiate the contract at any time that it is failing in its purpose. Eventually, the Able Underachiever ought to assume full control over what is being done away from school rather than having to rely on childlike treatment and checking up by parents who probably gain little satisfaction or recognition for this parental task.

Question for the reader

Can readers imagine other types of dialogue that Able Underachievers could be having with their parents beyond what is stated above?

We hear too little about really exciting, collaborative work on a preferred activity in which the parties interact together in a more mutually constructive manner as might be seen in camping, Scouts, coaching, playing music together, designing a website, travelling abroad, having an exchange student from abroad living in the home, etc. Where is the side-by-side joint progress towards a shared goal in areas beyond routine household tasks that might well not hold great interest?

What can be done to develop the relationships Able Underachievers have with their peers, siblings and parents to enhance achievement?

The two most significant themes suggested by the Able Underachievers themselves were a need to maintain their social identity at whatever cost and their desire to interact with their peers in lessons to receive and give peer support. To a lesser extent, Able Underachievers make reference to the value of sibling and parental support.

Social identity

A significant finding that came from the authors' study and was polar opposite to what they would have liked to have found was that affiliation with Able Achieving peers was seen to Able Underachievers to be disadvantageous. This was highlighted clearly in Table 1.3: Constructs influencing Able Underachievers (revised list) in Chapter 1. In looking for solutions, we might begin by reflecting on what we know about the Able Underachievers' perceptions of themselves and their perceptions of others in the school context in Table 3.1. The following must be read in the context

Table 3.1 The attributes of key players in the social and academic worlds of Able Underachievers as perceived by themselves

Attributes	Able Under-achievers' self-perceptions	Peers they associate with	Teachers they like	Able peers they don't associate with	Teachers they dislike
Mood	Relaxed	Relaxed	Balanced	Hard working	Stressed
Wit	Humorous	Fun to be with	Use humour	Serious	Use sarcasm
Skill at relating to others	Socially skilled	Popular and friendly	Warm, easy to approach	Perceived as geeks, spoffs nerds, swots or squares	Single out pupils, publicly embarrass
Talking	Enjoy conversing	Talkative	Find time to talk to pupils	Talk less, more compliant	Talk too much, shout
Allegiance	Loyal to friends	Trustworthy	Fair and respectful	Personally disciplined	Overly critical, negative
Ability of others	Value diverse ability among friends	Mostly average to below average ability	Instruct well, listen and encourage	Mostly Able Achievers	Don't explain well, don't inspire
Interests	Interests such as music, sport, art, cadets	Share similar interests with Able Under-achievers	Take an interest in pupils	Lack friends, limited social life	No personal interest in pupils
Support	Supportive of less able peers	Supportive of peers	Supportive of all pupils	Popular with some teachers	Favour some pupils over others

that these are the pupils' perceptions, some of which could be challenged by those who do not share their social world.

When questioned about what changes Able Underachievers would like to make in schools, there was some reference towards improving social relationships with teachers (some pupils considering it to be the responsibility of teachers to be more friendly and supportive towards them) but no indication on the part of the Able Underachievers of a desire to relate more to Able Achievers. There was no evidence from our interviews to suggest that the Able Underachievers had taken the time or trouble to get to know many Able Achievers and, therefore, they assumed they had little in common with Able Achievers on a social level.

What we do not know is the extent to which these Able Achievers (as cited by those interviewed) engaged in fun, non-academic activities outside of school and whether they were socially skilled or not. The evidence suggests that, on the whole, very able pupils have well developed emotional and social skills that often emerge at an early age (Gomme 2000, Freeman 1997). There is no reason, then, to suppose that Able Achievers do not share many of the social characteristics of Able Underachievers. What it does suggest is that the peer group culture reinforces certain stereotypes and subgroups to which you either belong or you do not. Therefore, if you affiliate with one group, then you can only make assumptions about what it would be like to affiliate with another.

So if there is little motivation for Able Underachievers to close the gap between themselves and Able Achievers then it is left to teachers to do the following:

- demonstrate that they value able pupils for their social and non-academic skills as much as their academic ability;
- challenge and dispel the myths associated with Able Achievers;
- develop a culture in schools in which Able Underachievers begin to collaborate with Able Achievers.

Valuing Able Underachievers for their social and non-academic skills
Teachers could find ways of exploiting the social skills of Able Underachievers in Personal and Social Education and especially through the new requirements for teaching citizenship. One hopes that educators will also recognise the importance of showing these skills in all aspects of school life and that their recognition will not be confined to the teaching of PSHE lessons. With new advances in our understanding of the importance of the personal intelligences, including emotional intelligence and emotional literacy (Gardner 1993, Goleman 1996, Sharp 2001), the need to recognise the importance of social and emotional skills is becoming more apparent. Able Underachievers have the skills and resources that teachers could use to promote this.

In addition to traditional curriculum areas, the arts and sporting achievements, pupils even at secondary level need recognition for their social and emotional skills and for perseverance, for creative ways of approaching learning tasks and for demonstrating independence and self-regulatory behaviour. Some schools, place as much emphasis on 'Code of Achievement' as on 'Code of Conduct'.

The need to address this area is all-important as seen in a recent example. The chef Gary Rhodes revealed in an interview for *Vivid* (Baker 2000: 36–7) that when he was at school he discovered that he could cook, but he felt that he could not tell any of his friends. As a result, nobody in school knew of his talents. His best friend was also doing ballet at the time, but it was not until they left school that they felt able to reveal their real interests and talents to each other.

Dispelling myths associated with Able Achievers

If both staff and pupils had a greater awareness of the interests and achievements pupils had out of school and these were publicly acknowledged and celebrated, this might not only increase the value of non-academic skills but might also begin to highlight some of the similarities rather than the differences between groups of able pupils.

In some schools, parents of new Year 7 pupils are asked to complete a questionnaire, indicating the interests and achievements of their children out of school. Form tutors could act quickly to encourage increased social networks of pupils with similar interests who may not know (or otherwise would never find out) this information. Social networks need not be restricted to pupils within the same form, year group or even school. Bailey (2000) recommends using technology such as e-mail to ensure the long-term success of such relationships. This approach is already used within the adult world where students have distance learning tutors and role models whom they access by e-mail in different countries. This process could be repeated with other year groups in recognition that young people's interests tend to broaden and mature as they get older.

To develop this approach further, staff could act as role models in deconstructing stereotypes, and could publicly celebrate their own diverse interests and achievements to stimulate others. Pupils hold some teachers in secondary schools in high regard generally. In one school the head of PE revealed to his pupils that he wrote poetry in his leisure time. We are generally not good at revealing the scope of our talents and interests to young people so that they move beyond perceiving us in one role and dimension only.

Fostering a culture of collaboration between Able Underachievers and Able Achievers

There are a range of government initiatives now promoting improved practice and provision for 'gifted and talented' pupils, for example 'Excellence in Cities', summer schools and masterclasses. These initiatives provide new opportunities for increasing collaboration between groups of able pupils. However, the identification and selection of able pupils for such provision is still not well defined. Research already points to the fact that able pupils from disadvantaged backgrounds, minority cultures and those with special educational needs (for example, dyslexic pupils) tend to be underrepresented in programmes designed for very able pupils (Bailey 2000). Where provision exists in schools, teachers need to consider equal access not just for pupils such as those mentioned above but also for Able Underachievers.

Schools are now increasing the practice of target grouping more able pupils to encourage them to work with like minds. However, there is evidence to suggest that many able pupils, by virtue of the fact that they are underachieving (and other factors), are not necessarily selected for inclusion in extension or enrichment activities. In making the distinction here between the two types of provision, 'extension' usually refers to the practice of the inclusion of more challenging tasks and activities within the classroom that are related to the curriculum. 'Enrichment', on the other hand, tends to refer to stimulating experiences that are usually on offer to some students outside of the normal curriculum and often outside the normal school day.

All young people need to feel that they belong to a social group in which they are accepted. The Able Underachievers questioned had very few experiences of being included in enrichment opportunities for able pupils within their schools, and therefore it can be inferred that they had lost opportunities to develop an identity with groups of achieving, motivated pupils who were more likely to be selected.

The point to be made is a warning to educators of the danger of limiting access to pupils who could potentially benefit from extension and enrichment opportunities. This can occur either because teachers feel that the pupils show little commitment to learning in the first instance or because they perform poorly on more formal measures of assessment through which they are selected. Whitmore (1985) warns that the over-riding problem for underachieving gifted pupils is the lack of provision for them to learn. What seems to be required in addition to making provision available to these pupils, is a shift in culture in schools so that more students want to emulate Able Achievers. If more students are actively encouraged to affiliate with Able Achievers and to access more stimulating forms of provision, Able Underachievers would most likely learn to value and desire opportunities to collaborate with groups of like minds. Where pupils in secondary schools already work in sets, an increase in pair and group work might well also have a motivating effect on the lower achievers in the group.

Julian Whybra (2000) outlines a range of extension and enrichment programmes, that include:

- Cluster grouping – *the practice of students from neighbouring schools meeting in a central location for short-term enrichment courses.*
- In-school cluster groupings – *opportunities for able pupils within one year group to work in a master class in one subject area (e.g. mathematics) with a teacher highly competent in this area.*
- Withdrawal programmes – *students withdrawn on fixed timetable or rotational basis to work with those of similar ability and interest in a small group setting (more likely in the primary phase).*
- Residential courses – *often occurring at weekends and in holidays.*

The above list is not exhaustive but demonstrates some options which, when evaluated, show gains in confidence, self-fulfilment, new friendships and new-found attitudes to mainstream learning among those pupils who have experienced such provision.

If Able Underachievers are to reduce the stereotypical views they hold of Able

Achievers then they need opportunities to mix with them in both academic and social ways. There is a need for Able Achievers and Underachievers to:

> . . . become more self-consciously aware of the beliefs which unite them and the differences which threaten good relationships with them . . . it is never more important than today, when the existence of cultural diversity among the members of a school community may be far greater than ever before. (Hulmes 1998: 160)

Peer support

Tough (1979) reminds us that children need to talk with one another to promote social development. Romaine (1984) goes further to describe the integral role of communication to the 'enculturation' of children and young people. She explains that it is through language learning that knowledge, skills, attitudes and aspects of culture are transmitted. By the end of their junior years, most children will have developed a range of social skills and sufficient forms of expressive language to initiate and sustain conversations with familiar and unfamiliar adults and peers (Locke and Beech 1991). However, pupils in adolescence need to continue to use language as a tool to explore and manipulate their social environment and establish their status and role relationships within it:

> . . . an increasing amount of socio-linguistic research on the structure of intra-group communication has revealed that one of the most important influences in the development of communicative competence is the style of speaking used in peer group interaction and the continuous monitoring from peers to which members are subjected. (Romaine 1984: 183)

There is little support for the view that children and young people gradually assimilate male and female norms of interaction from adult role models. Far more evidence suggests that much language learning occurs through peer interaction, even though children and adolescents are capable of switching from adult to peer codes. As language development is innate and follows a prescribed developmental path, it seems there are powerful motivational forces at large for adolescents who seek to be part of the culture and accepted within the peer group. In order to achieve this, it can be argued that some adolescents will exercise their need to have conversations with their peers at every opportunity, including during lesson time.

For the teacher, this poses challenges of classroom management and creates the dilemma of imposing controls such as the insistence on working in silence. Creating such working conditions, however, was generally felt to be uninspiring by the Able Underachievers in the study. Many of the pupils questioned would fall within the category of pupils who regularly chatted in class and were reprimanded or punished as a result. Discussion with the pupils themselves seemed to indicate that it was unlikely that these behaviours were deliberately intended to annoy their teachers, but that they stemmed firstly from the powerful pull of the peer group and secondly, from preferred learning styles.

Most of the students interviewed expressed a strong social identity with their peers and a sense of enjoyment and affirmation in associating with them. Teachers adopt their own strategies for managing this. When Able Underachievers felt most comfortable they identified teachers who would allow for a flexible approach, allowing some 'chatting' and discussion for parts of the lesson, provided that the objectives of the lesson were not sabotaged. In the case of other teachers, it was noted that they established a style of rapport that mirrored the linguistic style of the peer group (for example, as seen in the use of humour).

Secondly, those of us who have worked to understand and help children and young people with learning and/or behavioural difficulties are aware that there are many differences between people and many different preferences. Hartmann (1998) reminds us that some of us prefer high levels of stimulation, while others prefer quiet; that some people are mostly attracted to novelty and variety while others prefer routine, familiarity and structure. What was interesting to note about the young people in the study was that most of them preferred noisy classrooms and teaching approaches that involved novelty and variety. One idea in addition to the notion that pupils need to reinforce their social standing in the class group by talking at a social level with peers, is that they will create a degree of noise to provide the optimum condition in which to work. The downside is that they often do so at the expense of completing or attempting work to a satisfactory standard, or that they distract others who prefer quieter conditions in the classroom.

Other factors which result in the underachievement of these able pupils in lessons are also likely to be at work here. However, with respect to 'chatting', pupils desire to engage in it, but teachers tend to use less respectful communications to control it, such as shouting and sarcasm.

Schmitz and Galbraith (1985) talk about the need for very able pupils to have what they term 'comfortable classrooms' in which to work, where the teacher supports and encourages by providing clear expectations, constructive criticism, tangible rewards, structure, and time for sharing and relaxing. Wilcockson (1997) noted in an 11-year study that looked at underachievement in reading in a middle school, that it was noticeable that teachers devalued or underestimated the influence of school-based factors on underachievement. When able pupils develop behaviour patterns of lack of interest, effort and disaffection, these are more likely to be the symptoms of underachievement than the cause. Studies have shown that it is possible to reverse the effects of underachievement by modifying the learning environment to meet the pupil's needs (Whitmore 1980; Supplee 1990). When searching for causal factors, much seemed to hinge on the relationship between the pupils and their peers and the teacher, teaching styles and classroom organisation.

The points here also relate to the earlier suggestions in Chapter 2 of ways of developing 'teaching talk', but the emphasis on working in a more social environment appears significant. Some of the factors from Wilcockson's study influencing underachievement and relating to the learning environment are shown in Table 3.2.

Table 3.2 The learning environment (adapted with permission from Wilcockson 1997: 39)

While the pupils who gave their views in Wilcockson's study were a little younger

A good classroom	A good school
Working with friends	Lots of clubs
Group work	Not many rules
Having a laugh	Out of school visits
Being able to talk	Fair punishment
Getting good marks	Homework only if it is needed
Being listened to	No litter or graffiti
No favouritism	Space to play
Being trusted	
Being group leader	
Plenty to do	

than the students whose views were gathered by the authors, a lot of parallels can be drawn with the authors' findings and the statements in Table 3.2.

One way of resolving the situation then would be to make classrooms more relaxed and socially responsive environments where peer talk, in particular, is an integral part of the learning process. The Able Underachievers themselves would welcome an increase in the strategies mentioned below:

• being spoken to quietly by teachers;
• allocating a part of the lesson for social exchange;
• allowing low level 'chatting' during work assignments;
• greater use of debate and group discussion;
• peer tutoring – explaining concepts to others;
• pupils sharing ideas with a partner; and
• pupils listening to music (use of a personal stereo) while working.

Sometimes, in order to engage pupils more meaningfully in their learning, it pays to take risks and give them a degree of control and autonomy that some teachers are reluctant to do. Able pupils generally flourish under such conditions (Eyre 1997).

> Deci, Nezlek and Sheinman (1981) explored the relationship of teachers' orientations to children's intrinsic motivation and self-esteem, particularly with regard to autonomy/control orientations of the teachers. A striking feature of their results was that children's perceived cognitive competence, self-worth and mastery motivation were all greater in classrooms of autonomy-oriented teachers than in classrooms of control-oriented teachers. (Burden 1994: 315)

Vygotsky (1962) would argue that thinking aloud inextricably links language and thought. When a pupil takes over the role of the teacher in 'explaining', this will in turn enhance the depth of his or her own understanding. Therefore, the argument that able pupils are wasting their time helping less able peers has little credence, and approaches where pupils instruct others such as peer tutoring (Topping 1988) have been largely successful and are known to enhance both achievement and self-esteem.

Peer tutoring can take place with pupils of mixed ages. For example, Able Underachievers in Year 10 or upwards might increase their level of motivation towards their own studies if they were assigned the task of tutoring a young Able Underachiever, either generally or within a particular subject area. Conversely, an older Able Underachiever might benefit from being mentored by another pupil.

Sibling and parent support

What was interesting from the authors' study of underachievement was the value Able Underachievers placed on seeking support with learning assignments out of school from their siblings, many of whom they referred to as older Able Achievers. Such affiliation could be nurtured without endangering their social identity in school. With respect to parents, many Able Underachievers found them supportive as regards homework but generally gave few clues as to other ways parents influenced their achievements. They did make similar comments, however, to those made about teachers in terms of positive and negative experiences. Many of these relate to the way in which parents communicate with their Able Underachievers.

Csikszentmihalyi *et al.* (1997) conducted an extensive study of talented teenagers and concluded that the motivation of young people is deeply bound up with their social environment, including not only their peers, but also the influence and encouragement of their parents.

Much more could be done to enlist the influence of parents in meeting the needs of Able Underachievers. Often there is a deal of negative energy that could so easily be redirected if schools sought to develop these links further. At a local National Association for Gifted Children (NAGC) meeting the authors attended, much criticism was expressed by a parent of a very able pupil about the pupil's teacher.

The complaint was that the pupil was not being sufficiently challenged. In the case of pupils who are at risk of underachieving, other than the annual report to parents and parents' evenings, it would help if the dialogue between parents and teachers were increased, so that any targets, provision or achievements were made explicit.

It helps pupils to see their teachers and parents working together and developing what are referred to as 'nurturing communities' in meeting the needs of able pupils (Leyden 1985). The point to be made here is in connection to that made in the last chapter where the need for teachers to have facilitative conversations with Able Underachievers was highlighted. The same principles and types of questioning apply to parents. If parents (and perhaps also siblings) were encouraged to attend teacher–pupil consultations, not only could teachers model the types of questions that look for possibilities, but family members would be able also to contribute to the process and see the support mechanisms in place for the young person.

Summary

For teachers who are looking to develop the relationships Able Underachievers have with their peers, parents and siblings, the following key points represent opportunities for change:

- In closing the gap between Able Underachievers and Able Achievers, much needs to be done to challenge misperceptions and deconstruct the barriers that prevent both social and academic collaboration.
- The social and emotional skills of Able Underachievers could gain recognition within the new developments of PSHE and citizenship in the curriculum. Other non-academic achievements could be more widely recognised and valued.
- Able Underachievers will seek out opportunities to 'chat' and nurture social respect among their peers at the expense of focusing on their work. Classrooms could become more socially comfortable learning environments, allowing for increased social exchange, pair and group work and peer tutoring.
- Teachers could involve the parents (and possibly siblings) of Able Underachievers in joining teacher–pupil consultations where they can contribute to, and observe, the facilitative conversations adults can have in looking for possibilities for increasing achievement.

Suggestions for further reading

Bailey, S. (2000) 'Culturally diverse gifted students', in Stopper, M. J. (ed.) *Meeting the Social and Emotional Needs of Gifted and Talented Children.* London: David Fulton.

Freeman, J. (1997) 'The emotional development of the highly able', *European Journal of Psychology in Education*, XII, 479–93.

Sharp, P. (2001) *Nurturing Emotional Literacy.* London: David Fulton Publishers.

Thinking and learning with Able Underachievers

In this chapter the authors analyse and develop the comments that Able Underachievers made with reference to the thinking and learning factors that affect their academic progress. Chapter 4 starts with key points that came from the study, specific to the theme of thinking and learning (Figure 4.1) and ends with a summary of opportunities for change.

- Able Underachievers have no great love of learning in traditional academic subjects and show preference for social life and recreation, performance, hands-on practice and creative activity.
- They have little experience in school with bands, teams, clubs or groupwork but value adult-oriented work, for example being involved with the cadets. This is a lost opportunity as Able Underachievers do not seem interested in organising, or initiating for themselves any affiliation with, extra-curricular activities which could make school life more exciting.
- These pupils are bored by excessive copying, sitting passively, lack of variety, lack of relevance, dull lecturing, uninteresting topics, silence, waiting and poorly planned lessons. There is a power imbalance and Able Underachievers do not feel they own the problem or are responsible and empowered to do something about their underachievement and lack of interest in academic subjects.
- These young people do not readily identify activities in school that they consider to be positively challenging. In contrast, they dislike taking tests, meeting deadlines, writing long essays, working alone and facing up to new work in a topic area. These students do not see demands and challenges with associated rewards in school as exciting and welcoming.
- They might well work harder if expectations and standards were raised. Screening to find talent and subsequent mentoring with adults or peers might be helpful.
- Able Underachievers value diversity (such as multi-media work) in teaching and groupwork and prefer practical hands-on approaches involving performance other than predominantly listening and writing and they welcome research practice. They want to break out of the restrictions of closely controlled classrooms and be able to use more freedom and space in the way that students in higher education might be able to do.

- These students seem to have developed a limited repertoire of study skills that does not match their creativity, spontaneity or imagination. This area could be developed.
- These pupils see homework more as a burden than an opportunity. Some work gets done but it falls far short of what might be possible if the Able Underachiever was motivated and saw a better purpose to this work.
- These young people have some strategies to address boredom and poor concentration, but this area could be developed more using Able Underachievers' talents. Strategies seem short-sighted and not systematic or dynamic. Able Underachievers accept boredom as a major part of school life with some resignation.
- Able Underachievers claim the above strategies are partially successful. Able Underachievers need to open a dialogue with teachers and peers about problem ownership, causation and preventative interventions.

Figure 4.1 Key research outcomes relating to thinking and learning factors that influence Able Underachievers

Some of the influences resulting in underachievement that were highlighted in Chapters 2 and 3 by the Able Underachievers could also come under the heading of thinking and learning factors as they relate to the relationships and dialogue taking place within the teaching environment. This chapter seeks to highlight more specifically the influence of the curriculum and other learning opportunities accessed by Able Underachievers and the extent to which these may also contribute to their underachievement.

What the pupils had to say about activities that excite them

Q1. What gives you a buzz or excitement in and out of school?

This initial 'warming up' question was designed to encompass those activities which potentially might interest or inspire Able Underachievers in any environment. We wanted to know what grabbed the attention of Able Underachievers. Follow-up questioning directed the respondents back to school as a location if it was not mentioned specifically and spontaneously in the first response.

To some extent, the oral replies confirmed that the random selection procedure had indeed located somewhat academically disinterested students, as none of the 26 responses mentioned any great love of learning or enthusiasm to work hard at traditional academic subjects. The most frequently cited interest areas were PE or sports which were cited by 16 (62 per cent) pupils and covered activities such as:

- rugby
- football
- tennis
- swimming
- athletics
- sprinting
- cricket
- badminton

The exceptions were pupils who cited some interest in German and science as subjects.

The only other academic interests mentioned were by one pupil expressing a liking for asking questions in science and another who said:

Subject 11: Erm . . . just generally when teachers make the lessons exciting. You know it makes it easier to understand. Like err rather than just doing straightforward learning like they make a game out of it or something like that . . . Err just law and English . . . you could do some drama work to help you with your learning.

It was also encouraging to note the pupils' serious interest in 'hands-on' applied performance activity in creative areas, including drama, music, drawing, playing the guitar, computing and art.

Subject 4: I like going to the music room and playing the guitar there and I'm like free to use that with the music teacher.

Many students chose non-academic responses, indicating that their greatest thrill or excitement came from being with friends, playing, taking breaks, doing something new, talking, having a laugh, hanging out, etc.

Interpretation

This question failed to tell us much other than the fact that these Able Underachievers value recreation and social time generally. Traditional school subjects did not rate highly with them, except when they involved creating, performing or practical work. Perhaps this gives a clue to engaging them more widely.

Questions for the reader

Why does this group of potential achievers fail to rate highly activities that have been designed by their teachers to achieve academic goals?

Would we be more inclined to see greater engagement if somehow they felt some degree of ownership of the learning environment and of the curriculum itself?

How would we accomplish this?

How could we overcome the predictable resistance to engaging in academic subjects?

How could we get a discourse or conversation started on this topic?

If readers have any ideas, why not stop reading for a moment and write them down?

Q4. Have you ever had the opportunity to join an interesting activity or group either in or outside of school?

This question afforded the opportunity to talk about time spent on memorable or interesting activities by Able Underachievers either in or out of school. Ideally, we sought information on membership and enthusiasm for teams, groups, clubs, affiliations, bands, activities, etc. The picture emerging was one suggesting very little experience of group activity on a formal basis. The singular exception was that nine pupils (35 per cent) either were in the cadets or had been in the cadets at some time. This was not expected, as the Able Underachiever cohort showed little interest in affiliating with organised groups that were already up and running in their local areas. They did not seem well briefed as to what was available or how to discover this information.

The cadets are unusual in that they offer adult-oriented experience which requires a level of commitment and self-discipline. Perhaps that explains some of the interest that attracted this group to affiliate with the cadets and take up additional challenge in life. Pupils cited activities such as going on combat trails and assault courses, shooting, flying planes, learning drills, etc. which are outside the normal National Curriculum range of school-based work and involve physical exertion and an element of risk taking. It sounded more grown up. The stories told conveyed real interest and excitement seldom seen at school.

However, one pupil quit the cadets:

Subject 25: I used to do cadets but I did that for only about two or three weeks.

Interviewer: What was it about the cadets that made you want to quit?

Subject 25: Well they never got me any further. I couldn't really do anything. They kept me back for ages when everybody else was going forwards.

There were a few students expressing individual preferences for activities like:

- watching science lectures
- being in a sports team
- playing an instrument
- cooking
- attending a one-off event
- performing in a play or a musical production
- doing voluntary work with the elderly
- engaging in a hobby
- attending a youth centre

Interpretation

There was little awareness expressed as to whether more opportunities for activities or groups existed locally either in or out of school. When asked if a given activity such as a club (drama, debating, chess, computing, science, etc.) were to start at school, most did not demonstrate interest in attending. What should we suppose to be the motivating influence behind this rejection or indifference? Nor was there much interest shown by the pupils in trying to start up an activity in its absence. This raised further questions as to whether this was mainly a lack of interest on the part of the Able Underachievers or a feeling of not being empowered to innovate a school change. We recognise that lack of interest in joining structured activities among teenagers is not necessarily confined to Able Underachievers.

The overall pattern of responses did not demonstrate an enlightened school sub-population of Able Underachievers that is well versed in tactics and strategies to improve the school environment. In an ideal world we might at least have hoped that Able Underachievers would create their own group or activity, utilising their own creativity and needs as a driving force. Thus far this has not happened spontaneously among those interviewed.

Question for the reader

What would happen if staff took more positive steps to facilitate or resource groups and activities where Able Underachievers were left with the responsibility of getting it organised?

This would put the responsibility into the hands of the Able Underachievers who would have the most to gain.

Q5. If something really interested or excited you in school how would you develop this?

This question was designed to identify further details of known or planned activity that generated enthusiasm and even passion. The authors wanted to know what were currently in place as opportunities and what hopes and plans pupils held regarding the future, given the fact that the first three years of their secondary education were coming to an end.

The responses gained mirrored the findings of Question 1 about what gives these pupils excitement or a buzz. Virtually no one singled out a mainstream traditional academic area such as English, languages, maths, history, geography, etc. Those few who showed enthusiasm and initiative tended to focus on sport, practical activities and the performing arts. A great deal of this was located out of school or off the normal National Curriculum timetable. Much was focused on work being done or planned to be done more or less alone, such as doing research, visiting the library, trying harder, investing more time, persisting, etc. Some pupils indicated a need to talk with others, but this was mostly to seek help or advice from teachers. Other people in the schools were conceptualised as passive rather than showing great leadership or charisma in starting something.

The cohort did not mention much that would have involved organisational, systematic, motivational and selling skills. They seemed more likely to adopt a passive stance, suggesting that really there was not much going on at the moment. If something were to be started by others they might be inclined to 'give it a go' but this fell well short of self-organising ability or motivation to initiate a project that might result in the formation of some group activity like starting a club, a band, a team, a theatrical group or a project. There was no evidence of social risk taking here. There was no evidence of optimism that effort put into creation might have a payoff.

A few pupils cited current projects that were by and large organised by others. The authors did not form the impression that this Able Underachiever cohort felt trained, supported, motivated or even hopeful about launching something to supplement what was currently on offer at school. Obstacles were cited such as resistance among teachers, the need to be careful in deciding which teachers to approach, teachers being busy, financial limits, etc. Some had been involved in projects and later quit.

Interpretation

So far, we seem to have noted a pattern of lost opportunities which will be revisited later in the book. Many pupils can cite a singular event such as a school trip to an outdoor centre or a performance that was memorable, but these Able Underachievers do not seem to be able to initiate or to access regular extra-curricular activities that would provide an intellectual and nourishing challenge to them and harness creative energy that might raise their aspirations and standards within the National Curriculum.

What the pupils had to say about activities that did not interest them

Q2. What turns you off or bores you in or out of school?

This question was designed to elucidate further reasons for underachieving at school. Respondents were quick to identify predictable reasons for becoming bored such as:

- having to copy from the board or write excessively;
- having to endure repetition in talk and topics from teachers;
- having to read too much;
- having to address academic tasks that are inherently uninteresting;

- not having enough fun;
- having to be quiet or silent too often;
- not being able to do enough practical work;
- having to wait; and
- enduring unprepared teachers covering for absent colleagues.

Interpretation

It is hard not to identify with the voices of Able Underachievers who feel both aggrieved at their predicament and usually quite unable to see any simple resolution to being in a tedious classroom environment. They sadly appear accustomed to it. Conspicuously absent were voices of invention, imagination and empowerment in the face of an almost impossible situation. Some blame is attached by the respondents to both subjects and teachers. There seems to be an element of resignation that this is the way school is and always will be. There is not much compassion or understanding for the teacher who is responsible for the lesson. Students are quicker to identify uninspiring aspects of teaching and learning than to identify activities that are stimulating.

One forms the opinion that there is too much sitting passively and little or no credit being given for prior knowledge. There seems to be a lack of variety in curriculum delivery, or at least the pupils fail to identify it if it is happening. There seems to be something absent in the dialogue between these Able Underachievers and their teachers. Perhaps this simply reflects a perception of a power imbalance, but the result is a lost opportunity to communicate in an empowered way that might resolve the dilemma to the satisfaction of all parties. Every other student in the class might benefit if the Able Underachievers were more engaged and productive. It could give the class a morale lift and further stimulate and excite the teacher. Perhaps the other pupils are just more conforming.

It is here that the authors reintroduce the theme of lost opportunity which recurs throughout the reading of the pupils' responses to these 36 questions. It seems simple enough to postulate that the teachers have a problem and that the Able Underachievers have some solutions which they will not offer up for free to their teachers. Volunteering is not an integral part of their pupil–teacher script as they see it. Able Underachievers do not feel particularly inclined to volunteer solutions to their teachers. It is as if the pupil–teacher scripts were handed out or 'fixed' at some date in the past and cannot easily be altered. To do so requires an assessment of pupil motivation that has not yet been satisfactorily initiated and a 'safe' mechanism which allows for pupils and teachers to provide each other with constructive feedback through which both parties can gain.

Researchers and Ofsted inspectors might well not be surprised at the above opinions voiced by Able Underachievers. They might say this is not new: it has been said before. They might well feel they know what constitutes good teaching. Many of these suggestions should have been covered in initial training for teachers. What Able Underachievers contribute to the debate is that these positive teacher actions, values, principles and attributes might have been raised somewhere but they are not being seen effectively in action at school on a regular basis. The Able Underachievers just do not spot the types of teaching we admire often enough.

What the pupils had to say about challenge and expectations

Q3. When do you find the work really demanding or challenging in school?

This question did not seem to tap into the really positive and invigorating aspects of a challenge in school, where challenges should be welcomed and valued for their own sake. While four students (15 per cent) did cite challenges that they welcomed, most cited negative examples where the demands seemed unappreciated or unwelcome, such as:

- taking tests;
- having to perform;
- meeting deadlines;
- writing long essays;
- working alone;
- feeling pressured or confused; and
- having to face the responsibility of addressing new work in a topic area or project.

Preparing to take tests (revising), while unwelcome for some, was viewed positively by others.

Interpretation

For Able Achievers the use of demanding and challenging aspects of the curriculum might well provide great opportunity for rewards, praise, pleasure and satisfaction particularly when they have finished the work and it is positively evaluated. However, with Able Underachievers the pattern seems to be different. As we see, there seems to be some ambivalence about seeking out extra demands, perhaps because there is less personal history with success and its payoff.

If Able Underachievers miss out on the appreciated challenges and the subsequent rewards that could follow task completion, they are doubly disadvantaged. By inference and outside of this current research, the authors strongly suspect that Able Underachievers could actually derive considerable pleasure and self-satisfaction just from:

- participating in the struggle by overcoming obstacles;
- looking for clues amidst a lot of distraction;
- finding answers and solutions;
- solving puzzles;
- climbing mountains (figuratively);
- marshalling resources; and
- planning and executing a successful strategy.

Able Achievers perhaps do not need the external reward of public success, having found the activity of participating in a challenge to be rewarding enough. Our Able Underachievers may well be missing out on this challenging aspect of their education. If they actually do experience positive educational challenge they mostly fail to recall it when asked for examples. This is a lost opportunity.

Q32. Are the standards set for you high enough?

Some evidence suggests that Able Underachievers act and behave in the way they do at school because staff do not expect much more in terms of measured attainment on school tasks such as homework, essays and exams. There can be no doubt that what we see as attainment must be influenced by what we expect from students. This question sought a better understanding of just how these particular Able Underachievers estimated the standards expected of them, and also how they felt about raising these standards, which obviously would mean putting out more effort and work.

No one asked that the standards be lowered. Eight Able Underachievers (31 per cent) expressed the view that they would welcome having standards raised in respect of school work. The rest expressed satisfaction that the standards as set were adequate.

Interpretation

These responses show some separation or differentiation of views among the Able Underachiever cohort. Almost one-third were asking for their own personal standards to be raised. 'Who will do this?' was one response. To be fair this was a safe comment made to a visiting interviewer rather than to a member of the teaching staff, and it can be assumed that following the departure of the interviewer Able Underachievers most probably did not seek out a teacher and ask for higher expectations to be made. Why would we expect them to?

In terms of interventions it would be an achievable task and perhaps a good starting point in any secondary school to survey the Able Underachievers and try to identify the subset who would like higher standards to be negotiated. Some schools already do this with a mentoring system specifically designed to target this cohort, and offer comprehensive ongoing assistance with achieving higher standards by setting mutually agreed targets at school that require more effort.

Questions for the reader

Do you know what your school is doing about setting appropriate standards and targets today?

Do you know how often they are set and how they are recorded?

Are they negotiated with Able Underachievers and are their parents involved?

Are these standards or targets reviewed and do they achieve the desired results?

Do we know what the Able Underachievers feel about these standards and targets?

Is the role for parents (if they are involved) in setting standards and targetsclear?

Were you satisfied with the standards set for you while in school?

What the pupils had to say about learning and study skills

Q24. How do you learn best?

Research shows that there are different styles and preferences for learning. Investigations into the causes of underachievement conclude that the learning environment and a student's learning style are significant factors creating a potential mismatch between a young person's needs and his or her educational environment (Redding 1989, Carnegie Council on Adolescent Development 1989). We wanted to know what Able Underachievers (as a subset of the student population) specifically thought were the best individual conditions for school learning. The results suggest two conclusions. Able Underachievers value diverse teaching and learning methods. They also show a strong preference for practical and applied tasks instead of the more prevalent techniques that are overly characterised by listening, copying and writing.

They are attracted to school tasks described as:

- interesting
- fun
- entertaining
- well organised
- clearly presented
- unambiguous
- social
- relaxing

They really seem to welcome projects in which they can become involved in handling practical materials and make creations and products in a wider context than just with books, pens and paper. They value being able to experiment with materials and use practical applications of theoretical material.

Subject 11: I'm quite into Egyptology.

Interviewer: You've been into Egyptology for a long time?

Subject 11: Yes . . . quite a long time . . . there's this film about it and I'll rent it out even if like people say it's not very good.

Interviewer: How long have you been interested in Egypt?

Subject 11: Erm quite a while since I was about . . . say since I was about eight actually . . . just things I've read and things on TV and I just think it's really appealing.

Interviewer: Have you got anything about Egypt off the Internet?

Subject 11: Not particularly I mean if like I look in the encyclopaedia and look up vocational things and I'm quite interested in like the way that they built everything.

Here was an Able Underachiever making reference to video, television, reading materials and an encyclopaedia. He seemed interested in researching as a way to learn. Others made suggestions such as minimising revising before tests as it can interfere with memory. One (*Subject 1*) stressed the value of persisting by saying *'Just keep on trying and . . . try your best'*.

 Subject 17 said '*Um when you're actually doing work you learn better than the teacher just talking to you.*' Others stressed the value of working with someone else such as a group or a partner while some expressed preferences for working alone and teaching oneself. Perhaps these preferences are task specific and would vary depending on the task demands and the context in which the work was to be addressed. Some had no particular contribution to make to this question. One mentioned the use of revision cards. One valued being asked questions by his sister.

Interpretation

There can be no doubt that these Able Underachievers had already found alternative methods of getting work done, some of which had been available in school but not used often enough in their opinion. For example, Able Underachievers praised the occasional field trips from school as an innovation that broke the tedium of normal school life, stressing how different this type of experience was and wondering why the staff seemed unable to arrange these outings more frequently. As a group they did not seem to appreciate all the problems, challenges and risks that field trips can cause for teachers.

 As mentioned earlier, Able Underachievers seem to thrive in areas of performance where they can be active, energised, engaged and creative, with music, art, woodwork, metalwork, computing and cooking as examples. Even in science there can be opportunities in the laboratory to put thoughts into practice and introduce an element of individuality to the curriculum. Able Underachievers wonder why practical work seems to be used so much less frequently in other school subjects. Perhaps it is more about crowd control where the teacher sets the procedure for the whole class as an operating instruction, and Able Underachievers suffer more because of having less opportunity to use their own unique learning styles and preferences.

Questions for the reader

Think of your own preferred ways of learning and ask yourself how much you think your own achievements, vocation and areas of interest have been influenced by your own preferred learning style.

Able Underachievers do not describe classrooms as being stimulating places to learn new skills. If Able Underachieving pupils were convinced that their method (or learning style) worked best, what do you suppose the teacher would say in response to their request to use it?

Would you predict resistance?

How could this be overcome?

If you could talk to an Able Underachiever today as a mentor about your own preferences what would you say?

Q25. Have you developed your own study skills? If so, what are they?

Here we sought more information about any personal skills or methods that Able Underachievers have acquired either by copying them from someone else or by inventing them themselves. Unfortunately, the question did not produce the diversity and imagination that we had sought. It resulted in 14 Able Underachievers (54 per cent) stating that they could offer nothing in the way of a suggestion.

Those who made contributions offered suggestions like:

- looking for something novel in the task
- listening to music while studying
- relaxing
- reading
- being self-disciplined
- using the Internet
- testing themselves with a partner
- watching the TV while studying
- working in a quiet space
- revising
- making notes
- cue cards

Interpretation

The interviews with 26 Able Underachievers demonstrated a wealth of imagination and insight that they had about themselves, their lives at school and what seemed to influence their work habits and their resultant low attainments. Nevertheless, this question failed to spark that creativity. For example, no one individual pupil mentioned anything remotely involving having a conversation with someone like a mentor or adviser about their underachievement. No one offered suggestions here about restructuring the school or home environment to create a climate or culture that was more conducive to meeting the needs of Able Underachievers. These suggestions will, however, be addressed in later questions.

Study skills can be used in the classroom or else in the library or at home. They can make a great difference to academic engagement, motivation, recovery when stuck, relief when bored, persistence and task completion. The high proportion of pupils giving a nil response to Question 25 suggests the need for more explicit teaching of a range of study skills from which individual pupils could select and adopt those that matched their own needs and preferences.

Questions for the reader

What particular study skills do you prefer?

Did you discover them yourself or did someone teach them to you?

What would you have to say to an Able Underachiever who did not feel he or she actually possessed any unique study skills?

What could you demonstrate particularly to an Able Underachiever who had no positive Able Achiever role model and no mentor or the equivalent?

Q34. On average how much time do you spend on homework each night?

Thus far we have gained no quantifiable data that might shed light on actual work being done at home, or perhaps at school, as out-of-class preparation required by the teachers. Clearly some pupils see homework as an activity that can be done at school as well as at home. This question was mainly intended for descriptive purposes and cannot be used for comparison with Able Achievers as the data was not collected in this research exercise.

Caution is needed as time spent on homework is really a vague indicator. While it would be advantageous to know how much quality work was being completed outside of formal lessons, we sought and obtained the slightly less rigorous data of Able Underachievers' perceptions of how much time they were investing in these out-of-class assignments. We have no way to cross-validate the estimates for accuracy but the statements do provide another example of what Able Underachievers want to volunteer to this research project.

Two Able Underachievers (8 per cent) were unable to provide estimates here. The rest offered such a wide range of responses that it seriously challenged meaningful analysis and interpretation because Able Underachievers wanted to qualify their answers by showing that there was great variation in many cases from having no homework set to working all evening. However, when pressed for a numerical average based on five evenings per week, most produced a number ranging from nil to three hours. The average was about 50 minutes per evening. Eleven Able Underachievers (42 per cent) said they would do either 30 or 60 minutes per night on average. Four Able Underachievers (15 per cent) said they would average more than this. Several gave estimates that varied so much as to make the numbers look rather unreliable and more like a wild guess.

Interpretation

This question was only included to see if Able Underachievers did acknowledge that they were doing some out-of-class preparation. It is clear that some are actually claiming to be putting in the time. What we are missing is any evidence on what is being achieved qualitatively during these periods of time. Many Able Underachievers seemed ambivalent about homework, acknowledging it to be a burden rather than an educational opportunity in most cases. No one voiced any great affection for, or purpose behind, work done out of class. Many pupils worked with music or TV in the background and argued that this aided concentration or task completion.

Questions for the reader

What do you think about these estimates concerning homework?

Does it appear to be another lost opportunity, with Able Underachievers simply going through the motions without any great commitment or purpose behind what they do?

What do you recall about doing homework yourself?

Does the practice of setting homework need to change in some way so that it becomes more motivating and productive?

Q26. What do you do when you are bored or not engaged that helps to get you back to serious work?

This question was intended to help us understand better the strategies that Able Underachievers use when they self-assess that they are bored and off-task and perhaps in need of a 'recovery' or 'repair' strategy. Follow-up questions focused on two contexts: the classroom and homework. Able Underachievers were encouraged to address those circumstances where they find that concentration has lapsed, when their minds have wandered onto something other than the designated task that was supposed to be the target of their undivided attention. No one seemed to have any difficulty comprehending the meaning of the question or what was being sought in a reply.

Responses varied as one might predict. Several admitted to talking to themselves, giving themselves advice and encouragement or a pep talk and perhaps reminding themselves of the adverse consequences of not completing the designated task. Some sought tranquillity and quiet, while others valued the use of music or TV as a background element that could perhaps focus the mind. One used headphones to filter out extraneous sound and boost concentration. Several thought the idea of taking a break or otherwise relaxing during homework was an effective way to refocus after a brief time off the task. Some encouraged themselves just to persist and think of the advantages of closure on a given task.

One would draw. Another would study the behaviour of those who were working and not distracted. Some talked to friends. One tended to look for an enjoyable task as a way to help get back to less desirable work. Changing activities was sometimes found to help.

Interpretation

Able Underachievers fully know and appreciate the problems of letting boredom enter the workplace and interfere with the tasks in hand. Some have a few ideas about ways of coping once the problem is diagnosed but no one volunteered any systematic preventative measures that might anticipate the boredom and allow them to take steps to remove it or minimise it. Able Underachievers seem to take it as part and parcel of normal school or homework life without any great resentment or motivation to explore the problem more comprehensively. No one mentioned seeking out a peer, a parent, a sibling, a teacher or a mentor in order to discuss this, with a view to achieving some type of relief. There seemed to be a strong element of accepting this state of affairs. Able Underachievers are resigned to treating boredom as a constant rather than as a challenge. While they note the value of taking a break, they seem less concerned about the critical ratio of productive work time to break time.

Questions for the reader

What are your strategies to recover concentration, focused attention and earnest commitment to 'lock onto' task completion, especially in the face of competing invitations like entertainment, eating, socialising, playing, daydreaming, resting, etc?

Do they work?

Would they be of any use to Able Underachievers?

Is it helpful to believe that some set tasks are just not worthy of the time needed?

Should Able Underachievers tell their teachers that they are struggling to stay focused on a task?

What do you expect that the teachers would say in reply?

Is this a conversation worth having?

Who should start it?

Could it be constructive?

Who owns the problem?

Q27. Does this [strategy] tend to work?

This was a follow-up question about the effectiveness of the interventions suggested in response to Question 26. All 26 Able Underachievers agreed that their interventions or strategies did indeed work. Many, however, qualified their answers suggesting that they were not 100 per cent effective or that they worked better in some classes than in others, or that they worked 'most of the time'.

Subject 16: I just sometimes I just put my music on and not listen to no one and just get on with my work.

Interviewer: Is that just at home?

Subject 16: Yes and when sometimes when I'm at school and I'm bored and everyone's just talking to me and if I've got to do it say like if they say 'do it or you'll get a detention at dinner' I just turn my music on and do my work . . .

Interviewer: So you put your music on you listen with headphones?

Subject 16: Yes.

Interviewer: What kind of music do you listen to?

Subject 16: Just err pop style ones.

Interviewer: And you can concentrate while that's on?

Subject 16: Yes because I'm not turning round and talking to no one.

Interviewer: You just put your headphones on you're listening to music and you just do the work?

Subject 16: Yes.

Interviewer: And the headphones keep you from getting distracted by the other people?

Subject 16: Yes.

Interviewer: Does this tend to work?

Subject 16: Yes but sometimes you do get them taken off you because you're not supposed to have them but I always listen to music when I'm doing my work.

Interpretation

Able Underachievers have their coping strategies that help them concentrate and stay on task and, regardless of any criticisms that they seem short-sighted and tactical, these pupils have some confidence in their immediate effectiveness. If professional staff want to raise aspirations and output among Able Underachievers then it would appear sensible to open up a better dialogue and listen to them about how they deal with loss of interest in the work, especially the inevitability of it happening. They should work with Able Underachievers to better understand boredom and its causes, and to identify short-term measures and, most importantly, long-term or strategic measures to reduce the incidence of boredom at source rather than tackling it once it has set in. A factor other than that of interest in the task that is alluded to by *Subject 16* is the level of social distraction that exists in classrooms and the pull of the peer group to be 'sociable' that also mitigates against on-task behaviour.

What can be done to stimulate Able Underachievers' interest in learning?

The main needs that Able Underachievers identified in relation to thinking and learning were their desire for a more practical, creative curriculum, a need to be positively challenged and a need to further develop and apply effective study skills.

Developing a more practical, creative curriculum

Many of the Able Underachievers saw themselves as having talents in creative areas. This is perhaps no surprise when we find that there is evidence to show that creative underachievers often lack the motivation to engage in routine tasks (Supplee

1990). At this point it would be useful to refer to the National Advisory Committee on Creative and Cultural Education that was established to make recommendations to the Secretaries of State on the creative and cultural development of young people. In the Committee's report (DfEE 1999), they stress the need to recognise and promote young people's creative talents as a means of increasing self-esteem which, in turn, facilitates the raising of academic standards.

They also note that there is little time for teachers to realise their own creative capacity. The report makes mention of the Tandem Project which encourages teachers to do just that. This report concludes that 'if as teachers we aren't creatively and imaginatively alive/enlivened, we can't create, imagine and inspire, i.e. we can't teach. We can deliver, inform, police, but not teach (DfEE 1999: 156).

Creative and practical approaches in the classroom
While our Able Underachievers would place more emphasis on creative and practical subjects, they would also include more application of practical and creative approaches within the classroom. This finding provides an incentive to think about how traditional subjects are taught and shows that there needs to be more emphasis on creative teaching and learning opportunities. But how can teachers achieve this when the curriculum is so prescribed and so heavily weighted towards the improvement of literacy and numeracy skills?

De Bono (1999) stresses the need for more practical opportunities:

> Education is obsessed with literacy and numeracy. Yet 'operacy' (the skills of doing) is almost entirely neglected. As soon as a youngster leaves school that youngster is going to need operacy. The Socratic idea that 'knowledge is all' is nonsense unless it also includes the knowledge of doing. (de Bono 2000: 4)

One suggestion is that we need to reconsider styles of teaching and move away from curriculum content for the moment to consider the tasks, activities and media we can use in delivering the curriculum. We already know that our Able Under-achievers have a preference for practical, kinaesthetic and creative activities which, in turn, suggests that they are more kinaesthetic and visual learners as opposed to auditory learners. One way to test this out is for teachers to present activities in varying ways and observe whether or not this has a motivating effect on pupils. Many traditional academic subjects lend themselves more readily to auditory and sequential methods of delivery, yet a creative teacher will find ways of moving beyond the verbal and logical in delivering curriculum content.

Firstly consider Gardner's multiple intelligences (Gardner 1993) as set out below. Gardner proposed an alternative theory of intelligence in which he claimed that there exist several relatively autonomous human intellectual competencies that he termed multiple intelligences:

- verbal/linguistic intelligence;
- logical/mathematical/scientific intelligence;
- musical/rhythmic intelligence;
- visual/spatial intelligence;
- bodily/kinaesthetic intelligence;
- inter-personal intelligence; and
- intra-personal intelligence.

Whether we discount Gardner's theory of intelligence or not, we should recognise that good practice in teaching includes teaching that aims to use a variety of multi-sensory (multiple-intelligence) methods and styles in order to engage all learners. This knowledge is far from new, as the earliest philosophers point out: Aristotle says that 'nothing is in the mind that is not already in the senses'.

Preliminary questions for the teacher wanting to develop styles of delivery

Which of the 'intelligences' above and preferences are my strengths and which do I feel less comfortable with?

If I am profiling the styles, intelligences and preferences of an Able Underachiever in my class, would his or her profile be very different from my own?

Do I think the teaching and learning experiences of this Able Underachiever provide for his or her particular multiple intelligences (strengths)?

If not, what steps could I take to include different styles in my teaching that cater for the different preferences of this student?

If we are promoting the development of students' multiple intelligences, then teachers, particularly those in secondary schools, may need to include in their lesson planning the means of curriculum delivery and tasks that move beyond those that rely predominantly on mathematical-logical and verbal-linguistic intelligences.

In addition to teaching and learning that involves talking, reading, writing, answering questions, numbers, analysis and the following of logical processes, (verbal and logical intelligences), teachers should also consider addressing in their planning some of the questions outlined in Table 4.1.

To foster creativity, we also need to encourage young people in a variety of ways. Such teaching promotes flexibility. Teachers will need to celebrate occasions when students produce strange ideas ('wild is welcome!') and support them in coping with a learning situation in which the process may seem unclear or uncertain for a time. The following provide some examples:

- See and feel things in a different way – In teaching citizenship or RE consider: when is a wrong a right?

Table 4.1 Aide-mémoire for planning creative teaching approaches

---

Visual/spatial approaches:
Can I make greater use of colour, symbols, posters, drawings, models or other visual aids?

Do I encourage students to think about concepts in visual ways (e.g. colour coding, mind-mapping, linking abstract ideas to objects or by asking students to 'picture this . . .')?

Do I allow students to present information visually?

Musical approaches:
Can I include a musical dimension to teaching my subject, such as performance, song, rhythm or musical notation?

Do I allow students to present ideas using a musical medium?

Do I play background music while students work or allow the use of personal stereos?

Bodily-kinaesthetic approaches:
Can I make greater use of physical, hands-on approaches to teaching and learning (e.g. practical demonstration, movement, role-play, experiments and interviews)?

Do I provide practical materials for students to manipulate?

Do I encourage students to exercise, relax or move around during lessons? (It is a known fact that standing up for a moment provides a release of energy.)

Inter-personal approaches:
Can I make greater use of partner or group work to promote discussion, debate and reflection?

Do I allow students to collaborate on joint written assignments or in proof-reading each other's work?

Do I 'teach' students effective partner and group work skills by making the processes involved explicit?

Intra-personal approaches:
Can I develop the way I give constructive feedback to students on the way they think and learn and encourage pupil target setting?

Do I actively encourage students to give their views on the teaching and learning styles used in my classroom in order to accommodate their needs and preferences?

Do I require students to keep a learning log, to reflect on 'how they are learning' in addition to their Record of Achievement?

- Make the familiar new again – In teaching history pick the name of a street or town: make up a story about the origin of the name.
- Do it a new way – In teaching politics or economics: you are the new dictator of your country. What rules would you make for your people to ensure a healthy economy?
- Teach it a new way – In teaching science or technology: given a collection of ingredients, create a new product.
- Communicate in a new way – In teaching English or drama: devise a new form of dialect or sign language for use by an alien species.

(Adapted with permission from a paper on ways to increase creativity presented by Dr Lorraine Bouchard at the Council for Gifted Children World Conference, Hong Kong, 1995, and also presented at the Texas Association for Gifted and Talented State Conference, 1995).

Creativity is also a means of bringing more humour into classrooms. We should, in heeding the voices of Able Underachievers, encourage them to play with ideas rather than play around. Perkins (2002) said that 'wit and humour, especially kidding around, are good exercise fields for creativity. By its nature, humour invariably crosses conventional boundaries and breaks patterns.'

Increasing creative enrichment opportunities
The approaches outlined above are centred around classroom practice. In Chapter 3 the need to include more Able Underachievers in enrichment activities outside the classroom (especially where this would encourage their active collaboration with Able Achievers) was explored. Many of the enrichment activities being promoted for able pupils in recent months focus on academic tasks, for example master classes in mathematics. What perhaps is needed is for Able Underachievers to be encouraged to take part in enrichment activities of a more practical and creative nature.

If pupils were consulted about activities that excite them, particularly out of school, and provided with encouragement and opportunity to develop these interests in school they might become more intrinsically motivated to achieve more generally within the school context. Unless teachers have conversations with Able Underachievers concerning what they feel passionate about and try to foster these interests, it is unlikely that Able Underachievers will feel empowered to make explicit their extra-curricular skills and to develop them in school so that both they and other pupils can benefit.

Increasing positive challenge

In considering ways of increasing challenge and raising expectations, we should consider the need to teach thinking skills *per se* so that pupils are aware that they not only have different learning preferences but that they can learn to think in different ways. Positive challenge can be increased if pupils experience delivery of the curriculum that encourages a wide range of types of thinking and when they are given credit for and encouragement to think about *how* they approach a task as much as the marks they might gain for it. The use of peer support or mentoring can also be used to achieve this.

Programmes that teach thinking skills

Many educators have demonstrated that it is possible to teach thinking and to 'change children's minds'. The work of Feuerstein (1973), Lake *et al.* (1989), Lipman (1980), Adey and Shayer (1994) and Ashman and Conway (1993) provide examples. Such interventions have demonstrated that even very young children and young people at different stages in education can be explicitly taught effective thinking and learning skills. Some of these programmes have been additional to the curriculum; for example; *Instrumental Enrichment* (Feuerstein *et al.* 1980). Others have been integral to the curriculum, such as the Cognitive Acceleration through Science Education materials (CASE) (Adey *et al.* 1989), and approaches that can extend the Literacy Hour in primary schools such as *Stories for Thinking* (Fisher 1996). The effects on children previously deemed unable or underachieving have been dramatic.

The importance of utilising cognitive process teaching methods and providing positive feedback is recognised in the work of Montgomery (1984 and 1999). Montgomery developed an approach known as Developmental PCI (Positive Cognitive Intervention) in which higher order thinking and metacognitive skills (learning how to learn) are developed by teachers through the ordinary curriculum. One feature of this approach involves the teacher moving around to every pupil in the class saying something constructive about their work in order to move it on to a higher level, and commenting positively on the pupils' learning processes. Montgomery uses the phrase 'catch them being clever' which is one that teachers are likely to remember, especially if they have been exposed to the language of Assertive Discipline (Canter and Canter 1992), where phrases such as 'catch them being good' embody the philosophy of the approach. The rationale for such approaches comes from the belief that these elements of learning need to be made explicit and students need to be encouraged to reflect on and make connections between the products and processes in their own learning.

Other approaches, such as Student-Assisted Education (STAED) promoted by Roeders (1995), emphasise the need for learning to occur within a dynamic interdependent system which needs to be optimised to maximise achievements. Roeders set out to demonstrate the benefits of a within-classroom approach, in which the pupils assist each other by working actively in groups, multifaceted methods and materials are used to meet the needs of individual differences and learning styles and relaxation techniques are promoted. There are strong links here with our Able Underachievers requests for an increase in working with peers in the classroom plus their desire for more creative and practical tasks.

How is this pupil being intelligent?
There is still a tendency for us to rely mostly on pupil achievements as seen in standardised tests and exams in drawing conclusions as to how able or intelligent pupils are. However, able pupils are not a clearly defined group and Able Underachievers, in particular, are not always easy to recognise. Many studies have set out to provide models of definition and systems for identification. Some definitions are narrow, while others are more inclusive, which adds confusion for teachers in trying to apply a system of identification that will recognise all able pupils:

> Giftedness can come in several varieties. Some gifted individuals may be particularly adept at applying the components of intelligence but only to academic types of situations. They may thus be 'test smart' but little more. Other gifted individuals may be particularly adept at dealing with novelty, but in a synthetic rather than in an analytical sense . . . other gifted individuals may be 'street smart' in external contexts, but at a loss in academic contexts. Thus giftedness can be plural rather than singular in nature. (Sternberg and Davidson 1986: 9)

Even the notion of being 'test smart' is an ambiguous one as many tests are known to be culturally unfair and to disadvantage some groups of able pupils, for example, pupils with specific learning difficulties, motor difficulties or pupils with attention deficit disorder. By the nature of their difficulties these pupils will underperform on tests, particularly those that are timed and require competency in reading and recording skills. While the underachievement of able children with specific learning difficulties (dyslexia) has been recognised for many years, the link between handwriting competence and the underachievement of able pupils, particularly of boys, is now becoming more apparent.

Many secondary schools now take note of measures such as cognitive ability scores (e.g. CAT Tests) often administered in Year 7 and compare these with subject attainments to identify underachieving pupils for greater pastoral support. While this practice will identify some Able Underachievers, it does not take account of the fact that some young people will for the reasons given above underperform on the tests in the first instance or take action to mask their talents. It is also easy to assume that young people who perform well on traditional tasks are the most able in that subject. A counter-example would be mathematics, where it is known that some of the best mathematicians as adults have been found to be poor at computation. Other factors such as task commitment and creativity (Renzulli 1986), along with ability, are also known to be crucial to high attainment: 'It's not that I'm smart. It's just that I stay with problems longer' (Einstein).

What emerges from the issues surrounding 'recognition' of abilities and talents, is the notion that we need to look beyond traditional school subjects and consider how children learn. Whether we are devising a test or observing a pupil learning, instead of asking 'how intelligent is this person' in this area, we need to consider how is this person being intelligent (Valsiner and Leung 1994). This is crucial if teachers are to recognise all Able Underachievers and raise their expectations of this group. The term 'catch them being clever' can be qualified by highlighting the ways in which able pupils can show this.

There are many examples of geniuses who were slow to develop basic skills such as language and reading or who performed poorly when presented with traditional tasks in school. For example, Albert Einstein and Leonardo da Vinci were late in learning to speak, Agatha Christie and William Yeats struggled to learn to read, Benoit Mandelbrot (creator of fractal geometry) could not count well and Sir Winston Churchill was the lowest achiever in his form at Harrow. On the basis of such evidence, we cannot afford to neglect to realise the talent in our schools by failing to consider 'how children are being intelligent'.

In order to consider how a pupil is showing his or her intelligence, teachers can use checklists as shown in Table 4.2 to assist their observations.

One of the most eminent writers in the field of thinking styles is Sternberg. According to Sternberg (1997), thinking styles are preferences in the use of abilities, not abilities themselves. He provides many examples to demonstrate that children, young people and adults are often perceived as less able or intransigent if they possess a dominant learning style that mismatches that of their teacher, parent, spouse or employer. This view has serious implications both in respect to the recognition of talent and with reference to effective teaching and learning:

> If we don't take styles into account, we risk sacrificing some of our best talent to our confused notions of what it means to be smart or a high achiever, when in fact some of our smartest people and potentially highest achievers may only lack the style that we just happen to prefer. (Sternberg 1997: 160)

Sternberg describes thirteen different thinking styles, some of which are as follows:

- Executive style: preference for structure
- Legislative style: preference for diversity, being creative
- Judicial style: preference for analysis and evaluation
- Global style: preference for perceiving the big picture
- Local style: preference for working with details

Table 4.2 Characteristics of older more able pupils (*Cheshire Management Guidelines – Identifying and providing for our most able pupils*, Cheshire County Council 1996: 32)

Positive
1 May display musical/physical/artistic/numerical/mechanical or intellectual abilities of a high order
2 Shows initiative in setting and completing own goals
3 Can be original, creative or inventive
4 Leaps quickly from concrete to abstract, able to make generalisations
5 Shows advanced understanding and use of language
6 Reads rapidly, shows quick mastery and recall of information
7 May possess extensive general knowledge
8 Asks provocative, searching questions and shows concern over worldwide issues
9 May have a wide range of interests/hobbies
10 May prefer the company of older pupils and adults
11 Can see humour in the unusual, appreciate verbal puns, jokes, etc.
12 May enjoy the challenge of open-ended, problem-solving activities
Negative
13 May be absorbed in a private world
14 Prefers to respond orally while written work may be poor/incomplete
15 May appear bored and lethargic, lacking in motivation
16 Critical of authority, generally anti-school, may truant
17 May lack self-esteem and be intolerant of self and others
18 Can be abrasively humorous with an ironic perception of others' weaknesses
19 Able to manipulate others
20 May have difficulty relating to peers and teachers

> **Preliminary questions for teachers who want to consider differences in thinking styles**
>
> Which styles characterise the way you prefer to approach tasks?
>
> Can you think of different tasks that you do that require you to utilise different styles?
>
> If you are a teacher, which styles are more prominent in your teaching?
>
> Try experimenting with a different style and evaluate the results.
>
> How can you encourage pupils to recognise their own thinking styles?

Sternberg makes the point that people tend to demonstrate profiles of styles that will vary across tasks and situations. Success in problem solving for example is achieved as a result of being able to move between global and local styles of thinking. On the whole, traditional teaching approaches tend to favour executive, judicial and local styles of working. However, some young people demonstrate more effective learning through global and legislative styles. An example would be some very able pupils with specific learning difficulties who learn more effectively when information is presented 'from the whole to the part' rather than in a 'part to whole' sequential fashion.

West (1991), for example, describes the effective means of teaching maths backwards to dyslexic youngsters. Sternberg himself recounts his own experiences in struggling to learn modern foreign languages in school. As an adult, he successfully learnt Spanish as a result of having a tutor who used the method of learning by context. It was through reading and listening to natural dialogues that he was able to infer the meaning of the words from the text.

One technique that Barry Teare emphasises in his teaching is to encourage teachers to challenge pupils by giving them an answer and setting them the task of inventing the question.

Other writers who have researched the needs of able pupils conclude that some prefer challenging activities that require global processing of information (O'Grady 1995). If schools are truly inclusive they surely, therefore, need to adapt to the needs of learners and explicitly encourage them to increase their use of and ability to switch between different styles:

> An historical trace of the research in academic underachievement among gifted students indicates a trend away from describing underachievement in terms of maladaption on the part of the gifted underachieving students towards describing underachievement as a mismatch between a student's needs and educational environment. (O'Grady 1995: 31)

In order to catch pupils being clever we, therefore, need to present the right opportunities for pupils to demonstrate how they are being intelligent, as it is now acknowledged by key professionals in the field (Eyre 1997) that identification is best made through enhancing provision for all pupils. In providing these opportunities we also need to consider the ways in which pupils respond to them.

Levels of thinking

Our Able Underachievers also gave out strong messages that they found much learning to be easy and repetitive. In Chapter 2 the point was made that teachers need to ask different types of questions to stimulate different types of thinking and learning. This aspect of teaching has already been explored in depth in many texts, and models of thinking hierarchies such as those based on Bloom's Taxonomy (1956) have been applied to many different subject areas to promote thinking questions and differentiated tasks.

Bloom's Taxonomy presents a hierarchy of thinking skills, the higher levels of which can be used to devise different types of questions and tasks for able pupils within a subject area. In reality, all students should experience learning and thinking at all levels to ensure motivation and challenge. Examples of planning prompts for teachers applying Bloom's Taxonomy are provided in Table 4.3.

What we need to ensure is that teachers plan to encourage students, particularly

Table 4.3 Hierarchy of thinking skills based on Bloom's Taxonomy

Level of thinking	Question/task prompts	Examples
Knowledge (identification and recall)	List, define, identify, label, name, quote, define, recall	Describe what happened when we dissolved powder A in liquid B
Comprehension (understanding, ordering)	Describe, interpret, predict, summarise, retell	Explain how the main character in the book came to betray his family
Application (using knowledge)	Apply, demonstrate, experiment, relate, solve	If we lived in a world without much moisture, relate how this could change our lifestyles
Analysis (recognising patterns)	Analyse, separate, classify, connect, divide, compare, explain	Analyse the factors why some students experiment with drugs and alcohol and why some do not
Synthesis (creating, combining)	Combine, compose, formulate, invent, integrate, create, design	Design a new cost-effective and environmentally friendly form of transport
Evaluation (judging, concluding)	Decide, judge, recommend, convince, give a reasoned opinion	In a crisis such as a fire or a flood give convincing reasons why it is best to stay calm

able students, to use executive control process. Gagne (1973) refers to this type of thinking as that of 'synthesis and evaluation' as opposed to thinking directly related to curriculum content, which is often more typical of lower order thinking processes, e.g. knowledge, understanding and application. Many would argue that thinking related to 'analysis' also represents a form of executive, higher order thinking. However, de Bono (1999) stresses that if we are to equip students for the twenty-first century we must reflect on the fact that we have become a nation of analysts. Traditional methods are concerned with 'what-is?' thinking, which allows us to use our experience and learning to apply standard solutions to standard situations. What we also need to develop is 'what can be?' types of thinking. Such design thinking is dependent on perception, possibility and practicality.

As an example of synthesis and to equip teachers with a planning tool to stimulate thinking, the authors have combined Bloom's levels of thinking with Gardner's multiple intelligences to produce examples of ways of motivating pupils through thinking type and learning style as seen in the planning grid (Table 4.4).

Table 4.4 Integrated thinking skills/multiple intelligences planning grid

	Verbal/ Linguistic	Mathematical/ Logical	Visual/ Spatial	Bodily/ Kinaesthetic	Musical/ Rhythmic	Intra- personal	Inter- personal
Knowledge	Memorise facts	Recall the four rules of number	Make observations	Identify body parts	Listen and identify sounds	Explain three things about yourself	Name three attributes of a friend
Compre- hension	Explain meanings	Carry out an experiment in the correct sequence	Read maps and charts	Show how to use tools according to their function	Match sound effects to the beg/mid/ end of a story	Draw a time time line showing key events in your life	Take turns in carrying out a conversation
Application	Speak with confidence in different contexts	Solve problems	Complete puzzles	Teach a sequence of movements to others	Play an instrument	Work indepen- dently	Work co- operatively as part of a team
Analysis	Debate a topic	Perceive relationships between quantities and concepts	Draw a diagram to show connections (e.g. mind maps)	Compare the use of gesture with the use of speech in drama	Make a survey of musical preferences in one year group	Develop a profile of your own strengths and weaknesses	Resolve conflicts by recognising both perspectives
Synthesis	Play with words	Formulate predictions	Design a new product in 3D	Choreograph a dance routine	Compose the music and lyrics for a jingle	Generate two personal targets for development	Develop a new friendship
Evaluation	Discuss opinions	Justify the methods you have used	Rank art work for level of imagination	Judge an athletics competition	Review a piece of music for a magazine	Reflect on **how** you have worked	Explain how you feel to someone you like

Promoting effective study skills

There is some suggestion that more time needs to be devoted to the teaching of self-organisation and study skills to equip pupils with the demands they will encounter on transfer to secondary education (O'Grady 1995). In the same way that thinking skills need to be developed, effective study skills need to be taught.

Accelerated learning techniques

Firstly, consider the term *accelerated learning*, a technique first used extensively by Georgi Lozanov to promote thinking. This should not be confused with the term 'acceleration', which refers to the practice of fast tracking pupils through the system, such as by skipping year groups or sitting public examinations early. Accelerated learning attempts to stimulate neural activity in the brain by encouraging learners to make connections between different types and styles of thinking. What is meant by this is encouraging pupils to use centres of the brain that are thought to be more right-hemisphere dominant (such as imagination, pictures, images, rhythm, music and patterns) at the same time as those that are thought to be more left-hemisphere dominant (such as language, logic, numbers, linearity). While teachers can encourage this by using multi-sensory, multiple intelligence approaches as described earlier, pupils themselves can be taught accelerated learning study skills techniques such as the use of mind maps.

Mind maps (Buzan 1993) are a very helpful technique to support students whose learning styles are predominantly visual, and whose thinking styles are largely legislative and global. Many able dyslexic students fall into this category. Mind maps involve the key concepts and vocabulary of a topic being displayed on one page, with the inclusion of different colours and icons to emphasise connections. This technique supports the student's ability to memorise and recall facts and analyse elements of the topic, and assists creative thinking as new connections and possibilities can be easily explored. Some teachers have also found these techniques helpful when introducing a new topic or when assisting the student in applying the technique to note-taking, note-making and the revision of topics for examinations. Many adults also find mind mapping an essential technique to separate thinking from writing and to develop a structure and direction which makes the writing easier, faster and more enjoyable.

Student suggested study skills interventions

These suggestions came from the Able Underachievers themselves and their proposals cover a wide range of familiar activities as follow:

- asking and answering questions
- visiting the library
- revising
- seeking support
- practising new skills
- obtaining a good orientation to the task

- reading
- using encyclopaedias and the Internet
- drafting study timetables
- playing soothing music or seeking a silent place to work
- investing extra time on a subject
- quizzing a partner and vice versa
- taking a break
- making notes
- associating with more able students
- using cue cards

Many Able Underachievers allegedly use 'pep talks' and offer spontaneous advice to themselves:

- to persist with the task;
- to avoid or ignore temptation and distraction;
- to think about all the adverse consequences of not completing the work;
- to assert themselves with anyone who interferes with learning;
- to return to incomplete tasks (psychologists call this the Zeigarnik effect);
- to work alone in those cases where this is the best practice;
- to teach themselves to concentrate better; and
- to use information technology skills more appropriately if it helps with learning.

Able Underachievers already have a wide repertoire of strategies and tactics that they can use to boost productivity and reduce underachievement at school. Whether these suggestions actually are used on any regular basis is not answered by this study. However, this gives us a window into the mind of the Able Underachievers. It tells us about the tools and resources to hand, but we are still uncertain how much use is made of them or whether it would help if Able Underachievers were trained by demonstrations of other techniques such as mind mapping (as suggested above), mentoring, word processing, assertion, conflict resolution, problem ownership, etc.

Summary

For teachers who are looking to develop the thinking and learning skills of Able Underachievers, the following key points represent opportunities for change:

- Able Underachievers value the application of creative and practical approaches to all subjects. Teachers, therefore, need to bring aspects of creativity and variety into their lessons and in doing so recognise and promote the preferred learning and thinking styles of students.
- Able Underachievers need increased opportunities and encouragement to become involved in creative enrichment (extra-curricular) opportunities in school.

- The identification of Able Underachievers is best made through challenging curriculum opportunities and observations of how these pupils are demonstrating their skills by the ways that they approach these tasks.
- Able pupils need to be challenged to think at different levels, particularly at the levels of synthesis and evaluation. Tasks and questions involving different levels of thinking can be combined with different learning and teaching styles to cater for pupil preferences. This would help to avoid a mismatch between the students' needs and the way they are taught.
- Teachers need to encourage pupils to actively use a range of study skills, including the use of accelerated learning techniques such as mind mapping, if necessary promoting these by example and demonstration.

Suggestions for further reading

Adey, P.S., Shayer, M. and Yates, C. (1989) *Thinking Science: The curriculum materials of the CASE Project.* London: Thomas Nelson and Sons.

Buzan, T. (1993) *The Mind Map Book.* London: BBC Books.

DfEE National Advisory Committee on Creative and Cultural Education (1999) *All Our Futures: Creativity, culture and education.* London: DfEE.

Montgomery, D. (ed.) (2000) *Able Underachievers.* London: Whurr Publishers.

CHAPTER 5

Responding to personal and emotional needs

The previous chapters have sought to identify Able Underachievers' perceptions of how others relate to them, and their views about the curriculum in schools and other learning opportunities. This chapter is centred on the personal and emotional needs that affect Able Underachievers. In Chapters 2 and 3 we highlighted the fact that Able Underachievers are also affected by the personal and emotional needs of others. This will also be taken into consideration.

- Able Underachievers do not overwhelmingly feel that worrying is a major problem in their lives although a fear of failure or being compared with others is worth exploring. In contrast, these students are aware of the high stress levels experienced by some teachers (referred to in previous chapters as teachers who shout a lot and who are overly serious). They find it difficult to be motivated in these situations.
- Able Underachievers could achieve an even higher level of self-esteem if they accessed and used more of the under-developed talent that they possess in academic school-work.
- These pupils are skilled at talking about themselves in a self-critical way but this does not appear to lead immediately to successful interventions that might boost attainments. They admit to being responsible for a large measure of their under-achievement.
- These young people know that they possess talents, abilities, inventiveness and performance skills that are not particularly acknowledged or celebrated in school. They have mixed views about associated publicity and the peer culture's views on excellence needs to be better understood. The new National Curriculum emphasis on citizenship could offer an opportunity here.
- These students acknowledge that they underachieve in school. They can be identified and singled out for intervention such as mentoring and target setting, but we suspect they would value some recognition that they are not fully to blame for the problems.

- These pupils do have ambitions but a poor grasp of higher education and careers, neither of which seem to exert much pulling power in terms of commitment and motivation. Homework often fails the relevance test.
- These young people definitely seem discouraged and pessimistic about some teachers and about the possibility of schools becoming more interesting and stimulating. Nevertheless, they plan to change their ways and work harder in Year 10, mostly because of GCSEs rather than a new attraction to the National Curriculum.
- Able Underachievers know what they do differently from Able Achievers but do not feel totally responsible for the discrepancies. They think that teachers own the problem. They think Able Achievers are too conforming. Unless some teachers change their perceptions of Able Underachieving pupils and the way in which they relate to them, these students are unlikely to do much themselves in terms of raising standards. We are stuck with the *status quo*.
- These pupils acknowledge their intelligence but often do not find school challenging. This is a lost opportunity again. Able Underachievers can provide evidence to back up their claims to be good at learning. They are not being overly challenged at school. Their low attainments must follow decisions about not making more commitment. Perhaps they do not see the pay-off.
- These pupils know they are good at learning and can summon evidence to prove this. They acknowledge a lack of commitment to achieving better grades.

What the pupils said about the influence of stress on their achievements

Figure 5.1 Key research outcomes specific to the theme of personal and emotional factors that influence Able Underachievers

Q18. Do you think that worrying interferes with your learning in school?

We wondered if Able Underachievers were inclined to worry a lot about their work at school and so this question was used to prompt for signs of anxiety. The group was almost evenly split on this issue, with half saying that worrying was a problem that caused interference while the other half did not think that worrying constituted a serious problem. While many admitted to worrying a little, they did not see it as something that needed to be addressed seriously. Two of the most frequently cited examples concerned revising for tests and getting work completed on schedule. Understandable worrying was mentioned in reference to bullying.

Subject 16: They like torment them if they get top marks . . . you know what I mean like saying 'You're a big head' and things like that.

Interviewer: Do you think that there's any way we could change the attitudes in this school that students have about clever pupils?

Subject 16: No.

Interviewer: If you saw your friends teasing pupils who got good grades is there anything we could do to stop that?

Subject 16: Yes . . . put them in detention and that . . . because it's like bullying really.

Interpretation

Much has already been written about the role of anxiety and how it can both facilitate and debilitate effort and motivation in school work. We wanted to see just what type of contribution worrying makes to Able Underachievers, as they perceive it. Some adults would argue that worrying is what keeps us on the 'straight and narrow' with our heads down and delaying gratification until the tasks are done. Others suggest that worrying, especially when excessive, just interferes with meaningful learning while also diminishing self-esteem and morale.

As regards our cohort we cannot say at this point that the whole group are worriers who need to have their anxieties assessed and resolved. Several seem to be handling worry in a mature way and are certainly not seeking help from adults with its management. Some manage to underachieve without paying too high a cost psychologically at least as far as self-reported worrying is concerned.

In contrast, we take a moment at this point to cross reference to Chapters 2 and 3 to Able Underachievers' responses to Question 7 (what teachers do that causes Able Underachievers to dislike them) and Question 28 (what would make Able Underachievers work harder). The Able Underachievers relate that they pay a high price in relation to their motivation and achievement because of the level of stress and tension displayed by teachers in some classrooms.

What the pupils said about their personal attributes

Q16. What do you like about yourself?

Self-esteem is an important factor in studying the motivation of pupils at school. This question was intended to investigate and describe how the Able Underachiever perceived his or her own strengths both at school and elsewhere in life. We wanted to ascertain what made each Able Underachiever feel proud of his or her accomplishments and successes.

While it is acknowledged that pupils tend to adopt a practice of being a little reluctant to make self-serving statements about themselves, these Able Under-achievers in the cohort interviewed did manage to answer the question and identified a wide range of actions that made them feel good about themselves. Only two failed to supply a skill or an attribute in response.

Responses included being good at playing music, sport, art, science, geography, maths, English, metalwork, woodwork, drama and computing. Two pupils could play the guitar well. One was learning to pilot a plane, and the cadets were cited again as an area where good work was taking place. Pupils were proud of some of their achievements. Several pupils rated themselves positively for attributes and characteristics such as:

- being comical
- having an imagination
- being friendly and having friends
- being non-judgemental
- having good sense in dressing

Others focused on learning skills, claiming to be good at writing, having good study and work habits, hitting deadlines, working at their own pace and being 'more or less good at everything'.

Interpretation

Despite all the other problems that Able Underachievers may have at school they do not appear as a group to have seriously diminished self-esteem or to have adopted an overly negative view of their capacities or their potential. They mostly seem to realise that they possess ability and could perform to a high standard in at least one area of their lives. With the exception of the two who were either very modest or who lacked something to be proud of, the rest have had experience of excelling with something, knowing the effort required and appreciating how it feels to demonstrate competence either privately or publicly.

So, these Able Underachievers are generally familiar with both working hard and feeling proud of what they have done, even if this experience has been infrequent or rare in their lives. They do not report problems with diminished self-esteem. So why does this experience not lead to a higher level of daily commitment to work at school on the curriculum? It is not as if we are speaking to Able Underachievers who have had no exposure to hard work and recognition. They just have little appetite for more of the same at school.

Questions for the reader

Are you convinced?

Do you need to know more about how Able Underachievers perceive themselves?

If so, how best could you achieve this?

Q17. What do you dislike about yourself?

This is a parallel question to the previous one. Six felt unable or unwilling to volunteer a response to it. The rest were quick to identify areas, usually one or two, where their own self-assessments made them conclude that they disliked something about themselves. Some cited their progress in specific subject areas such as French, history, geography, religious education and languages. Some mentioned habits such as:

- being forgetful
- not trying hard enough
- getting into trouble
- having bad handwriting
- messing about
- having poor concentration
- getting low grades
- talking in class
- having teachers on their backs
- not listening
- being off track

Some mentioned physical attributes like their hair or their height and weight. One complained of being too shy.

Interpretation

These responses taken with the previous ones in Question 16 show a group of Able Underachievers who have the ability to look carefully at their own repertoire of attributes and behaviours and comment constructively on their own strengths and weaknesses. We felt their answers were open and honest, conveying a sense of balanced and constructive self-assessment generally, and a willingness to see that at least some of their underachieving might be due to actions within their own control.

Q33. Who would you be inclined to blame for your underachievement?

Throughout the study the authors' curiosity about responsibility for under-achievement was raised by the responses of the Able Underachievers. The Able Underachievers were, therefore, asked whom they would blame for them not making the desired effort and gaining the marks or grades that they were capable of achieving. When pupils were not sure what answer to give, they were offered the usual range of possibilities, including teachers, friends, parents, siblings and themselves, or a combination of these.

Three Able Underachievers (12 per cent) did not want to blame anyone. Fifteen Able Underachievers (58 per cent) were inclined to take personal responsibility for their own underachievement as their first choice. Five Able Underachievers (19 per cent) blamed their friends or other pupils while three Able Underachievers (12 per cent) blamed their teachers. Respondents were also given an opportunity to cast a second vote for someone else to blame other than their first choice. Four (15 per cent) chose themselves, five (19 per cent) blamed teachers, six (23 per cent) blamed friends and one (4 per cent) blamed a parent.

In combining the voting for both first and second choice the rating looks like this:

Self	19	(73%)
Friends and others	11	(42%)
Teachers	8	(31%)
Parents	1	(4%)

Interpretation

Despite the conclusions reached earlier in this summary, with a lot of evidence supporting an external locus of control, the Able Underachievers questioned were quick to take the blame themselves for their low attainment in school. They had been particularly critical in earlier responses about all that was wrong with school, and the fact that a lot of lessons were of limited interest to them. Yet here, towards the end of the interview, they seemed to want to re-establish control over the process and claim personal accountability rather than blame someone else. It is interesting to see how little parents or siblings were seen as potential scapegoats when it came to blaming someone.

We are coming to the end of the Able Underachievers' voices that underpinned this investigation. It was most encouraging to see these Able Underachievers accepting a good deal of personal responsibility when accounting for their individual underachievement. There is great potential for assertion and action in owning a big share of the problem rather than wasting time blaming others exclusively which could leave them feeling passive and helpless. These Able Underachievers were going to the heart of the problem and were probably inclined to attribute the blame for their weak work productivity to themselves.

Questions for the reader

As the reader do you now want to apportion the blame or responsibility for Able

Underachievers' output?

Does the act of blaming or holding accountable help the situation?

Q19.   What characteristics do you feel you possess that are not valued by your teachers, friends, or parents?

From the start it was suspected that Able Underachievers bring into school a reservoir of talent and resources that teachers and the peer group and possibly their parents may fail to appreciate and value for a variety of reasons. This question was included to help us understand the scope of this lost opportunity and the reasons why Able Underachievers might have hidden talents and experiences that they are reluctant to publicise in school, perhaps for fear of the adverse consequences of calling attention to oneself and then acquiring a negative social label.

Eleven (42 per cent) did not make any suggestions, possibly deliberately or out of modesty, or because they had no real contribution to offer, but the remainder did. Able Underachievers claimed special abilities with:

- playing the guitar
- archery
- canoeing
- acrobatics
- running
- throwing
- table tennis
- rugby
- flying
- singing
- computing
- football

These responses show a bias towards performance with arts, recreation and sports rather than more traditional academic subjects or more personal characteristics. However, one pupil valued his sense of humour, another conversational skills, another self-confidence and a fourth rated general intelligence. In each case Able Underachievers felt confident that significant others were not really aware of these skills and abilities.

Subject 3: I can fly a plane.

Interviewer: What kind of plane?

Subject 3: Bulldog . . . they are ex-RAF mission planes.

Interviewer: Do your teachers know it?

Subject 3: No.

Questions for the reader

How do you suppose the teachers of this pupil would react to hearing this?

Would knowledge of this skill by the teaching staff support other learning opportunities in the school for this pupil and others, or encourage teachers to reframe their perceptions of this Able Underachiever?

Interpretation

No one voiced any great complaint at the social injustice of having talents that were unnoticed. Many exhibited a sense of pride in accomplishments that were not fully broadcast to the wider social community especially at school. Some of this may just be a part of the cultural expectation of having 'British reserve' which suggests successful acquisition of adult values in Great Britain. But there must be some costs involved to both Able Underachievers and the school in general when ability remains unrecorded. Schools that celebrate success through Records of Achievement, Able Pupil Registers and by having an explicit Code of Achievement are working to counteract this tradition in the hopes of raising standards and changing the host culture. This is so that being successful publicly is seen as socially desirable and valued throughout the community.

Questions for the reader

Can readers at this stage recall important personal accomplishments outside of school that were not publicised within school?

With hindsight was this satisfactory or would it have been better for the teachers and/or other pupils to know more about what was accomplished?

(Here we do not just mean an act of great heroism or being a national champion, we are referring to more normal accomplishments like learning a skill or overcoming an obstacle in life.)

Q20. Do you believe that you are not really working up to your ability? How do you know this?

This was a validating question used to support prior evidence that each Able Underachiever being interviewed was actually a pupil nominated by standardised testing, teaching staff and parents as an Able Underachiever who acknowledged this description as fair and accurate. The responses all confirmed that those being interviewed (100 per cent) considered themselves to be underachieving in one way or another. It is noteworthy that several did not mention this as their first response.

However, on reflection, they all did agree that at least in some areas of the curriculum they were not working up to a standard they would describe as acceptable or appropriate to their ability. The follow-up question ('How do you know this?') produced a variety of responses suggesting Able Underachievers are receptive and responsive to self-assessment and external evaluative feedback from teachers and peers about school competence and output. In other words, when they say they are not working up to their ability they can back up the assertions with explanations such as:

- not trying hard enough
- getting bad grades
- disappointing themselves and others
- finding someone to blame

- not concentrating
- expressing a dislike for a subject
- being distracted

Subject 7: Well for instance last year in science I was like top in my class even though I was in the top group and I was like getting sort of As and A*s but this year I've got a different teacher and he just doesn't recognise your potential and he just doesn't do anything to help you at all and the other did and he helped me as much as he could and he really, the other teacher, doesn't.

Interpretation

The findings here are helpful to the project because they do tend to confirm that the pupils selected for interviewing were willing to talk about, and were appropriately experienced to speak on, this sensitive issue of underachievement. It helps that Able Underachievers can answer this potentially painful question honestly and contribute to a further understanding of their unmet educational needs. For the record we should indicate that some schools make a point of identifying Able Underachievers early. These pupils are then given specific voluntary coaching and mentoring with the aim of setting and achieving educational targets that are designed to lift the Able Underachievers out of that designated category to become Able Achievers wherever possible. Teachers using these approaches showed great enthusiasm and optimism for them when talking with the interviewer as part of this research activity.

Questions for the reader

As a reader do you recall underachieving yourself at school?

Would you have been willing to acknowledge this when you were in Year 9 or in the middle of your secondary education?

If you would have made the honest acknowledgement that you were underachieving would you have been open to looking at your own under-performance and the reasons for it or would you have preferred to have been left alone?

Can you recall a teacher or other adult who made a significant difference in either reducing or enhancing your achievement in any area? What did that person actually do?

What the pupils had to say about the future

Q35. Do you have any plans to attend college or university later in life?

This question was included to see if Able Underachievers completing Year 9 of the National Curriculum were in any position to share particular long-term education hopes, or plans for the time after leaving school, or share some ambitions that might motivate better work habits and raise expectations.

Three Able Underachievers (12 per cent) were certain that they did not have a plan while 12 (46 per cent) did express a definite plan to go on to higher education either at a college or a university on leaving school. The rest felt uncertain but considered it a possibility for the future. Those wanting to pursue a particular course cited preferences in the following fields: science, business, music, graphical design, computing, maths, engineering and law. Three wanted a career in the RAF, including two who would like to be trained as pilots.

Interpretation

The responses suggested that this cohort of Able Underachievers did have some ambition although the pupils did not, at that point, have the understanding that would eventually come from subsequent careers interviews. This ought to provide further ideas for those planning school-based interventions for Able Underachievers. Perhaps if these pupils had a better idea at an earlier stage in their education of what might be possible, it would serve to motivate the Able Underachievers in the ways Able Achievers are already attracted to school tasks. This group certainly attached great importance to relevance, and anything being asked of them in school that failed to pass the relevance test was bound to attract less sustained effort in terms of task completion.

Questions for the reader

How important is ambition?

Would it make any difference if work shadowing, work experience, careers interviews, university visits, etc. were made available earlier to Able Underachievers who are looking for greater relevance in their studies?

Would this be just a waste of time in your opinion?

What would be more appropriate for those lacking a plan?

Q36. If I were to come back and see you in a year would the situation have changed? Would you be working harder?

This was the final interview question that was asked usually after about 20 to 30 minutes of dialogue. It was intended to see just how optimistic Able Under-achievers were in terms of their educational future. Almost without exception, Able Underachievers offered reassurances that if these same questions focusing on underachievement were to be asked at the same time next year these Able Underachievers would be working harder and achieving higher academic standards.

They tended to attribute the predicted redoubled efforts to the fact that in Year 10 they would be pursuing a GCSE curriculum requiring the taking of more courses that involved chosen options while simultaneously dropping some disliked courses. Some made reference to career plans and the hopes of getting a good job where success at school would be a requirement. One had aspirations to be made a prefect. Another optimistically thought that the teachers would be more encouraging. One thought he might *'not have the boring teachers next year' (Subject 26).*

Interpretation

Perhaps these Able Underachievers were just trying to present the interviewer with a rosy or glowing prospect for the new year coupled with overly optimistic aspirations and exaggerated good intentions. We will never know for certain, but once again the voices of Year 9 Able Underachievers are telling us something of the way they view the world around them. Perhaps those teaching staff seeking to raise standards among Able Underachievers can somehow take advantage of these personal predictions and plans rather than viewing them cautiously or cynically. Even if only some of these Able Underachievers actually return in the autumn sincerely hoping to work harder in the coming year, this intention could well inform the dialogue between teachers and pupils in setting targets for improvement in study habits and standards. It might help as well if parents were also involved in this dialogue.

Questions for the reader

Are you convinced about the good intentions of these Able Underachievers to work harder the following year?

Can they do it?

Will they do it?

Will assistance be needed?

If so, what type of assistance among those ideas already suggested by Able Underachievers do you think would be most helpful?

What Able Underachievers said about their commitment to learning

Q21. What do you do differently from other students in school who achieve at a higher level than you do?

We were seeking an assessment of just how perceptive Able Underachievers are at identifying what they do differently from their Able Achieving peers in the same school. It might have been predicted that Able Underachievers would tend to be defensive and to minimise whatever differences existed, or that they might claim that Able Achievers were smarter or more capable or more inclined to subordinate their lifestyles to the dictates of the teachers. We have already heard complaints from Able Underachievers about 'teachers' pets' or teachers who show favouritism towards more compliant or conforming students.

On the contrary these Able Underachievers were apparently honest and straightforward in offering hypotheses to account for differences in measured output on schoolwork. They admitted to:

- writing less
- being less compulsive in meeting deadlines
- revising less
- working less hard
- being more easily distracted
- having more fun
- doing less homework
- working more slowly
- thinking less
- talking too much
- concentrating less often
- working at a slower pace

Interpretation

These opinions suggest that Able Underachievers are quite skilful at seeing what their own actions or lack of appropriate actions costs them when it comes to measured school attainments. There was a clear trend to look at their own behaviours rather than just to focus on what the Able Achievers did in school. Responses were given freely without much resistance and in a detached manner. We did not detect any significant signs of regret, remorse or a guilty conscience. On the contrary, the responses came over more as mere journalistic reporting of facts, as if these differences were an acceptable part of school life. There was no hint of aspirations to move from the *status quo* to a new lifestyle where the gap between the performances of Able Achievers and Able Underachievers would be reduced.

In terms of future interventions to boost attainments, this objective detachment would have to be further explored and addressed. However, if Able Underachievers could be motivated to change some aspects of their lifestyles and put in more effort, they would not need convincing of the merits of holding themselves responsible for their underachievement. They already acknowledge that they do not try as hard or employ the study habits of the better-functioning Able Achievers. They seem to know what they and the Able Achievers are doing differently, but perhaps they exaggerate the social costs of working harder and hold somewhat inaccurate stereotyped opinions of the Able Achievers' lifestyles, which they ought to re-examine. Able Underachievers often portray Able Achievers as leading a dull, boring, over-conforming, isolated existence. Perhaps this needs challenging.

Questions for the reader

If you were an Able Underachiever in school, what did you do differently from the Able Achievers in your classroom? If you could go back and revisit yourself in the classroom what advice would you offer to yourself?

What might have shifted your thinking and, more importantly, your work habits and output?

Would you agree that you could have chosen to work harder but just did not want to do so?

What might have made the difference to your thinking?

Would it have been a special teacher, a mentor, a better Able Achiever role model, more self-confidence to follow up your own interests with less concern about the social consequences, membership of a group, or what? Be honest here if you feel that literally nothing would have made a difference.

If you were an Able Achiever at school, would you concur with the stereotypical view that Able Achievers lead dull, boring, over-conforming and isolated lives? Did you naturally affiliate with a broad cross-section of peers in school or were your affiliations more with Able Achievers and/or adults? What would have made a difference to your learning and social experiences at school?

Q22. Do you think in general that you are good at learning?

This was another question seeking confirmation that Able Underachievers are able to perceive themselves as able, clever and intelligent pupils. Predictably, there was very little difference in the responses of the 26 Able Underachievers surveyed. With the exception of only one, who was a little self-critical, the entire cohort acknowledged being 'good at learning'. They expanded on this notion by highlighting the fact that many school tasks were easy and could be done quickly. Some did not find school tasks hard, suggesting a lack of adequate challenge in their curriculum. Some expressed a liking for learning.

Interpretation

It helped to know that we were working with self-confessed Able Underachievers who realised and appreciated their own learning and memory strengths, despite the fact that underachievement patterns had resulted in their being selected to be interviewed. It was not too late to be talking with them. Their self-esteem had not been sufficiently damaged by underachieving to have left them with diminished self-concepts when it came to general learning. Many were able to back up these assertions with arguments as to why they responded to the question affirmatively. The statements were compatible with the selection procedure in which standardised testing, teachers and parents identified candidates to be interviewed. In terms of future interventions, these Able Underachievers did not need convincing that they are indeed able.

We can conclude from the Able Underachievers' responses that some have been insufficiently challenged in school. Year 9 is a pivotal year in which Able Underachievers can no longer just sit back and rely on their higher level skills in thinking, memory and recall. What they actually do or fail to do at this point makes a noticeable difference and this continues to be more serious with each passing year.

Questions for the reader

Who owns the problem of some pupils not being challenged in school: the Able Underachievers, the teachers, the teacher trainers, the authors of the National Curriculum, the peer group, the local community, etc.?

What did you do when you were under-challenged in school or even later in life, for example in your work?

Were you inclined to own up to this?

Did you find someone to blame?

Did you feel relieved that you could coast for a while?

Did you think it would last forever?

Who could have made a difference in your life?

Could anyone have entered the classroom scene and influenced your work patterns?

Could you possibly have challenged yourself?

Or, more radically, could you have entered into a dialogue with your teachers about the absence of meaningful challenge, or would this have been too risky?

Who would have known about this?

What might have gone wrong?

What would this intervention undertaken by yourself have cost you?

Q23. How do you know that? (that you are good at learning)

This was another back-up, validating question seeking further clarification as to just how confidently the Able Underachievers had responded to the previous question where they admitted to being able. Again, Able Underachievers spoke up affirmatively with explanations as to how they knew they were able or good at learning. The trend seemed to be for the Able Underachievers to indicate how fast or quickly learning was done. Several said they found learning to be easy. One *(Subject 11)* said he '. . . *liked a challenge*'. Several claimed to have a good memory. Several said their performance on tests served as proof of being good at learning. One felt able to pass on the benefits of learning to an adult. One hinted that the learning seemed almost automatic.

Interpretation

Again the Able Underachievers were confident in summoning up arguments which confirmed that they knew they were good at learning. There was no indication that the work at school was a great struggle or that they were avoiding work because they found it too burdensome. So if these Able Underachievers were putting less effort into task completion it seems it was not because the work was too hard or that the Able Underachievers lacked the intellectual resources to complete work to a high standard. We must look elsewhere to find better explanations to account for substantial school underachievement. Able Underachievers seem quite capable of grasping the relationship between hard work and good results. Low attainments must follow decisions not to make a commitment to work hard and achieve one's potential.

Questions for the reader

Do you feel the responsibility for underachievement is always a personal one or does it belong elsewhere?

How do you know when you personally are not achieving according to your own potential?

Do you trust these interviewed Able Underachievers when they say they are aware of their own abilities?

What can be done to address the personal and emotional needs that affect Able Underachievers?

Recognising and alleviating teacher stress

Stress can be both positive and negative, but when we are under a high degree of stress this will affect our emotional stability and ability to relate to others in positive ways. Teaching with the threat of performance related pay, achievement league tables and learning with the emphasis on improving test results, forces the classroom environment into one that fosters competition rather than collaboration. Add to this the constant revisions to the curriculum, the degree of prescription regarding curriculum content, the regular cycle of Ofsted inspections and target setting. With this difficult mixture, it is no wonder that within teaching there is a recruitment problem and a move to exit the profession in droves because of the stresses involved. Lawrence (1999) notes that recent studies show that teachers are now more at risk of developing stress symptoms than ever before. This in turn is hard to disguise in the classroom and soon interferes with the building of positive relationships. Some research 'has shown that a class will soon learn whether their teacher likes them, cares about their output, or feels they are inferior creatures, without a word being spoken to them' (Lawrence 1999: 40).

Many public and private sector services are beginning to look at organisational stress because of the effect this has on motivation, health, job satisfaction and most importantly for pupils in schools, relationships and productivity. A starting point would be for teachers individually or as part of supervision to consider the questions below.

Questions for the teacher

How does work make you feel?

What is it about work that makes you feel this?

How do your feelings about work influence your relationships with colleagues?

How do your feelings about work influence your interactions with pupils?

If you feel that you are stressed, what steps could you or senior managers take to reduce this?

While we can individually reflect on our levels of stress and how they affect our relationships with others, Sharp (2001), based on his recent work in Southampton LEA, highlights the need for education managers working within LEA services and schools to assess and develop their levels of 'emotional literacy'. This, in turn, Sharp claims, will significantly improve the degree of work satisfaction and productivity of teams and individuals working within those organisations. Emotional literacy is a term that is often linked with emotional intelligence. In the literature there is some disagreement over the terms used but considerable overlap as to what constitutes core competencies:

- self awareness
- emotional resilience
- motivation
- interpersonal sensitivity

- influence
- decisiveness
- conscientiousness and integrity

(Sharp 2001)

Sharp argues that organisations from senior management downwards need to recognise their strengths and weaknesses in these areas, both collectively and individually, in order to promote health, work satisfaction, enjoyment and increased attainment. If, as teachers, we do not take time to reflect on our own emotional strengths and needs, this will impact on the level of productivity within the organisation where we work and on our long-term health, well-being and performance.

This is an important point to consider if schools are to develop the curriculum according to new government guidelines on PSHE and citizenship, and also if teachers are to encourage a culture of achievement that permeates all areas:

Nurturing emotional literacy begins with the self and through individual development comes collective and societal change for the better. (Sharp 2001: 99)

If we accept the challenge that promoting our own emotional literacy makes us fit for the purpose of helping others to promote their emotional literacy, then the really hard choice is about whether or not we commit to action . . . to work on our self. (Sharp 2001: 91)

Such things as emotional intelligence do not come as a curriculum package which can be told to pupils and reinforced in worksheets. It arises out of the everyday interactions between people . . . One significant adult can make a difference. All children need such mentors but especially the underachieving and disaffected. (Montgomery 2000: 190)

Recognising needs

Firstly, we need to consider why it is that despite having relatively good self-esteem and having the skills and honesty to recognise their own failings, these pupils continue to underperform in school. One explanation comes from what has been termed 'Self Worth Theory' (Covington 1992). In order to protect their self-worth, there will be some circumstances in which a young person will stand to gain a great deal by not trying. This can result from negative feedback or peer pressure, and can also be a direct result of labelling.

In a study of Able Underachievers (O'Grady 1995) the pupils spoke of their embarrassment and of feeling stupid in class (particularly a class of Able Achievers) if they let it be known to the teacher that they did not understand something or if they felt 'put down' by the teacher's response to their incorrect answer to a question. Another explanation is that Able Underachievers tend to feel more comfortable taking the middle ground and associating with pupils less able than themselves, because they can maintain their position with minimum effort. It is clearly more challenging to be around high achievers and fail, leading to diminished self-esteem. Finally, for some able pupils having been labelled by adults as 'gifted', the very idea of trying to live up to such a label (possibly running the risk of failure if they try hard to do so) is enough to cause them to deliberately underachieve.

> Thus here emerges from this complex interplay among students, peers and teachers a 'winning' formula in the anticipation of failure that is designed to avoid personal humiliation and shame on the one hand and to minimise teacher punishment on the other: to try, or at least appear to try, but not too energetically and with excuses handy. It is difficult to imagine a strategy better calculated to sabotage the pursuit of excellence. (Covington 1992: 78)

There are still very few texts written on the subject of the emotional needs of able pupils, but Stopper reminds us, in the introduction to a recent book edited (2000), of the significance of the affective component of learning. We are also reminded of a 'differentiated model of giftedness and talent' (Gagne 1991) in which social and emotional factors are acknowledged. Gagne further stresses the critical impact on achievement and the development of talent brought about by significant adults, such as parents, family members, teachers and other role models. If these factors are so significant, then we must consider the affective component in having facilitative conversations with Able Underachievers.

Based on the literature in this field, the experience of the authors and comments of the Able Underachievers themselves, we would offer teachers the following suggestions which can be linked to the 'pupil–teacher' consultations that take place out of the classroom, suggested in Chapter 2:

- acknowledge the feelings of the young person and indicate that you care;
- talk about abilities and talents, both strengths and weaknesses, and avoid labelling pupils as 'gifted';
- praise pupils for skills and behaviours that are non-academic so that you present the message that you like the person for who they are and not who you would like them to be;
- in conflict situations, always listen to the young person's views and respond in a

way that is fair (compared to other pupils) and be prepared to compromise;
- encourage greater efforts and avoid showing your personal disappointment.

If parents are also involved in pupil–teacher meetings, the teacher can help moderate situations where the effects of labelling (described above) are obvious.

We, therefore, need to recognise the individual needs of Able Underachievers. We might also need to consider if any of our Able Underachievers have special educational needs for which they need support, or help with specific study skills. The Able Underachievers in our study, for example, expressed difficulties in the areas of concentration and writing skills. Unless teachers take the time to find out what is difficult for learners on a regular basis, they are unlikely to modify their teaching to take account of this (for example, allowing the use of Dictaphones, laptops for some pupils or teaching pupils to record and revise using mind maps.)

When we talk of having 'facilitative conversations' with Able Underachievers we would want to discourage the notion of 'counselling' *per se*. Counselling, used extensively in schools in America as an intervention with disaffected young people, has on its own been found to be of very limited use in reversing underachievement (Picozzo 1982, O'Grady 1995). The best 'facilitative conversations' are, in our view, likely to be those that teachers of Able Underachievers have with them on a regular basis, and which make a difference to the relationship these pupils have with their teachers. This, in turn, affects how these pupils respond within the learning environment. Discussions should make reference to pupils' experiences in the classroom and beyond. This does not detract from the fact that able pupils along with all pupils, may experience emotional or social problems for which they may wish to seek counselling from either professionals or peer counsellors if these exist in their school.

Lee-Corbin and Denicolo (1998) highlight the types of pupil–teacher interactions that militate against pupil achievement, one of which is the teacher's failure to take a personal interest in the pupil. It appears to be common for teachers not to be aware of the types of activities and achievements a young person has out of school. Sadler (2000b) questioned all the teachers of Able Underachievers in her study and not one could describe any interest that engaged the pupil out of school and, surprisingly, this was the case even for the teachers of Able Underachievers in infant and junior schools. The same finding emerged from the authors' present study in which some Able Underachievers had sporting, musical, computing and flying accomplishments of which they were proud. In most cases these achievements were not celebrated, known about or exploited in the school context.

In considering the needs of Able Underachievers, caring for them on a social and emotional level is a significant one. George (1992) was one of the first in the field to truly promote, through his own literature on able pupils, the need to consider the 'whole child', and he stressed the importance of self-esteem and self-actualisation.

Promoting self-actualisation

Earlier in this chapter we noted that our Able Underachievers did have ambitions and wanted to leave school with higher achievements than would have been predicted given their performance at that stage. Maslow (1954), in his hierarchy of human needs, placed 'self-actualisation' at the highest level. All individuals, if they are to be fulfilled in life, need to gain a sense of satisfaction that they are able to realise their own goals. One outcome of a pupil–teacher consultation may be to assign a mentor to the Able Underachiever to assist the pupil in realising his or her own goals.

The practice of mentoring in secondary schools is now becoming more common, but still many Able Underachievers miss out on these opportunities because they expend just enough effort to get by without being noticed. Montgomery (2000) calls these pupils RHINOs (Really Here In Name Only). Mentoring can take many different forms and be delivered by different types of people. It involves individual time spent with the Able Underachiever, usually by a teacher or adult in the community. The time can be spent helping the young person identify his or her barriers to learning and helping him or her devise personal targets in order to raise achievements in certain areas.

A mentor for an Able Underachieving pupil could also be someone who has a shared topic of interest, who could help develop the pupil's interest and depth of understanding of that topic. If the interest is a shared passion, this adult might also act as a role model, providing the pupil with encouragement that can increase his or her expectations and motivation in other areas. In schools where this practice is well developed, the pupil plays a major role in determining the focus of the meetings. Where the needs of the pupil cannot be met by the mentor alone, the mentor can facilitate further provision by helping the pupil making connections with others who can. Relatives and other adults within the community can also act as mentors, but it is usually more successful if mentoring is conducted by adults other than the young person's parents.

In some secondary schools, staff act as mentors for very able pupils in the feeder primaries. This can help to establish good relationships early on and to avoid some of the problems of boredom and repetition of the curriculum that can be seen among very able pupils in Year 7. It also allows for greater flexibility in cases of very able pupils who have exceeded the skills and resources of the primary sector in a particular subject area in Years 5 and 6.

Able Underachievers can be further encouraged to engage in self-assessment. Where good practice is seen in secondary schools, pupils keep learning logs in which they record observations about how they approach tasks, how well they work with others and how they feel about their learning. Working with 'response partners', a peer in the same class who can provide constructive feedback, can assist pupils in considering these matters. Pupils need to develop the skills of 'metacognition' in order to understand how they learn best and in order for them to become focused on improving their learning performance.

Involving parents and the local community

The Able Underachievers questioned in the authors' study attributed little responsibility to parental or sibling influences for their level of achievement. Yet Able Underachievers do value their parents and siblings if they demonstrate ability in assisting them with homework tasks. If we wish to encourage Able Underachievers to associate more with Able Achievers we need to consider the part that family, culture and community have in influencing achievement. A number of studies reflect such influences.

Csikszentmihalyi *et al.* (1997) looked at the self-reports of over 200 talented teenagers in a five-year longitudinal study. In this research, the authors explored young people's responses to questions such as, 'Why do some young people become disengaged with their talent?' They concluded that motivation is the key to the development of talent, and that high academic achievers work harder and are more self-disciplined than others, but that they are not necessarily born smarter. They found that the degree of motivation in young people was deeply bound up with their social environment, including cultural influences and their relationships with peers, parents and teachers. With respect to thinking and learning, students must feel that they have something unique to contribute and that teachers, parents, siblings and others recognise and value their individual skills. 'Excellence cannot be idiosyncratic, it depends on the recognition and approbation of a community. Hence the ideal must involve a struggle to express one's individuality in ways that are meaningful to others' (Csikszentmihalyi *et al.* 1997).

Butler-Por (1987) noted that, in addition to a pupil's self-concept and school experiences, parental, cultural and societal factors also contribute largely to achievement and underachievement. Likewise, Leyden (1985) writes extensively of the influence of the family and community on the healthy development of able pupils. More recently, Stopper (2000) edited a collection of articles entitled *Meeting the Social and Emotional Needs of Gifted and Talented Children*. One of the main aims of this book is to highlight the complex relationship between the intellectual, social and emotional development that affects an individual's achievement and fulfilment.

It can be difficult to modify attitudes towards achievement that may exist within a local community or to encourage a cultural shift within the peer group, even if these are needed to promote the achievements of some able pupils (Kellmer-Pringle 1970). However, more could be done to encourage parents to become more involved with their child's learning. Parents of able pupils often become detached from the young person's learning tasks when they leave primary school and become more independent. If parents are encouraged to take a more active role in homework assignments, projects and research by modelling, assisting and learning alongside their child, this can have a powerful effect. Further, teachers can assist by helping pupils network with adults in the local community, such as those in higher education and in local businesses. It is also helpful for pupils to see their teachers and parents working together. In short, there is a need to develop what are referred to as 'nurturing communities' in meeting the needs of able pupils (Leyden 1985).

Promoting intrinsic motivation

A key concept affecting achievement is known to be that of intrinsic motivation (Deci 1988; Passow 1990). It is not enough, however, to believe that teaching process skills to promote thinking and learning is sufficient: learning needs to be an emotional and interactive experience if it is to be intrinsically rewarding to pupils. Education, said W. B. Yeats 'is not the filling of a pail, but the lighting of a fire.'

Teachers who are passionate about their subject area can often inspire pupils with a love of learning for learning's sake. However, many of our Able Underachievers lose interest in learning, not necessarily because of the subject content, but because of the way that it is delivered and also because of the emphasis on what teachers and society value. We know that our Able Underachievers preferred creative and practical activities. It is possible to teach traditional subjects in creative and practical ways yet there seem to be fewer opportunities for this as pupils get older. Sternberg (1997) argues that we can talk of children losing their creativity in school, but what they really lose is the thinking style that generates creative performance. Freeman (1996) also notes that scholastic achievement requires a degree of emotional restraint, whereas a degree of emotional freedom is needed for the development of creativity.

The authors noted the distinct lack of will that existed among the Able Underachievers in their study to 'change the system' in any respect. Perhaps they felt that there was no point in discussing their real interests and preferences with their teachers or their parents or carers if they had experienced learning environments from an early age that placed value only on conformity and recorded achievements.

Able Underachievers are likely to achieve more if they perceive adults in their academic world on a more sociable level. This does not mean that teachers or parents have to become 'pally' with their pupils or young people at their own social level, but that a culture of mutual respect should exist. This is clearly not the case when you stop to consider the attributes of teachers that pupils are critical of, namely those which imply an avoidance of positively relating to Able

Underachievers and the exertion of power related to insisting on the production of academic outcomes. Mongomery (1999) also makes this point, stating that in many UK classrooms, pupils are being exposed to the pressures of extrinsic motivation and are 'made to learn'. She points out that this has the effect of reducing the pupils' ability to be autonomous and to self-regulate their learning. However, pupils need to be motivated to learn intrinsically and, as learning has an affective component, it is hard to see how achievements can occur without there being a positive relationship between the young person and his or her teacher or mentor. This is an important consideration that is overlooked in some learning situations. Boys appear to be particularly at risk in this respect as they are more influenced by the 'human relationships' aspects of teaching (Hymer 2000).

Chapters 2, 3 and 4 provide many ideas for promoting teaching and learning styles that would help encourage intrinsic motivation. The point to be made here is that if learning in secondary school classrooms allowed for more emotional and personal experiences then this would go a long way towards meeting the needs of Able Underachievers.

Summary

For teachers looking to address the personal and emotional needs that influence Able Underachievers, the following key points represent opportunities for change:

- Schools and local government as organisations might do well to consider how to address the level of stress and self-esteem of staff as a precursor to promoting levels of pupil achievement.
- Able Underachievers value teachers who develop a rapport with their students, who take a personal interest in them and who encourage and reward. Pupils' individual or special educational needs (for example, writing difficulties) should be addressed.
- In addition to school experiences, parental, cultural and societal factors contribute to a large extent to levels of achievement. Teachers should work closely with parents to ensure that pupils are valued for themselves and not just for their academic achievements.
- The social and emotional skills of Able Underachievers are now more likely to gain recognition within the new developments of PSHE and citizenship in the curriculum. Beyond this, teachers can enable pupils to experience a more personal and emotional response to learning *per se*. The use of learning logs would be an example of a way of promoting this.
- Teachers can help Able Underachievers gain access to adult mentors, who can nurture pupils' specific interests and provide ongoing support and encouragement.

- Parents can be encouraged to learn or study alongside their sons or daughters. Links with other adults in the community can be sought (for example, through higher education establishments and local businesses) as part of a network to support and inspire Able Underachievers.
- The able young student whose preferences, interests and creativity are largely ignored is likely to become an Able Underachiever, indifferent to school life and lacking in intrinsic motivation. An increase in recognition is required.

Suggestions for further reading

Sharp, P. (2001) *Nurturing Emotional Literacy*. London: David Fulton Publishers.
Stopper, M. J. (ed.) (2000) *Meeting the Social and Emotional Needs of Gifted and Talented Children*. London: David Fulton Publishers.

CHAPTER 6

Creating opportunities for change

We conclude the book with a final chapter designed to assist those who would like to further tackle the underachievement of able pupils in schools. This process is likely to raise attainments among all pupils and, therefore, is inclusive in its nature. We begin by addressing the last two questions given in interviews to Able Underachievers.

What the pupils said about how they would study underachievement

Q29. If you were to design a new school course and ways of teaching it that would inspire you, what would it be like?

This was an invitation to create a utopian school setting without needing to worry about how it might be created or what it would cost in terms of effort or money. Able Underachievers were given a licence and encouragement to be as imaginative as they wanted to be with this unusual task.

Only two (8 per cent) had no comment to offer. Able Underachievers offered a wide range of practical suggestions that were consistent with views expressed earlier in the study. They would have liked school to be more enjoyable and fun while working within an organised, controlled and disciplined setting with assertive teachers. Some wanted the noise reduced and again some saw value in having music available selectively. Some would have liked to see more interactive relationships and one specifically stressed the value of personal relations with teachers saying: *I'd have a lot more 1:1 to make sure people erm would be taught properly and make sure they actually understood what they were being taught . . . Erm try to be a friend to them'* Subject 9).

Many were really averse to the rules about silence and did not see why more group work and informal talking with friends within a class could not be accepted more readily by teachers. Again there were calls for more practical work and applications involving 'hands on' performance instead of the more traditional restricted routines in classrooms.

Subject 12: It would probably be making them actually do it instead of writing on sheets and stuff like building and putting like things together like.

They suggested that steps be taken to achieve a more relaxed atmosphere with bright, colourful and well-resourced classrooms with lots of computers and other high-tech equipment. A leisure centre built next door would be welcomed. One asked for '. . . *more art, more PE lessons, more trips out sometimes . . . more practical stuff, more woodwork' (Subject 19)*. They would have liked more options and variety at school.

One wanted no newly qualified class teachers while another specifically favoured younger teachers '. . . *who you can like talk to' (Subject 22)*.

Interpretation

Once again we see that Able Underachievers are in a privileged position to help us design more appropriate teaching environments for the new millennium. They tell us stories that can make it easy to remember what it was like when we were in school. But it is painful to think that Able Underachievers continue to complain that too many of their lessons are taught in under-stimulating classrooms by teachers who fail to address their needs. No doubt if readers of this book were to visit some of these pupils in school they would be able to see for themselves just how valid the claims of these Able Underachievers are.

All too frequently during the interviews Able Underachievers told carefully constructed stories of being bored that seemed plausible and reasonable. These pupils sadly had grown accustomed to this aspect of school life. They did not hold out much hope that anyone was going to take their suggestions seriously but that did not stop them from making the comments that they did make.

Questions for the reader

What would your utopian school look like and how would innovations be created and implemented?

What changes in the light of what you have read so far would you like to see operating?

Q31. If you were studying underachievement what question would you ask students? I'd like you to answer your own question.

This was a sweep question added towards the end of the interview exercise to use the skills and insights of the Able Underachiever cohort to assist us in this research. Basically, we wanted to know if they had any further suggestions to offer that might elucidate the causes of underachievement or what steps could be taken systematically to reduce or minimise its influence in schools.

Five Able Underachievers (19 per cent) did not feel able to provide an additional question for someone else at this stage of the interview. For the rest, the results suggested that the previous 30 questions had covered most of the subject under investigation. If the Able Underachievers had been doing the research interviews themselves with other pupils they would want to know why the interviewee was underachieving at school. Their own explanations about causation tended to focus on:

- subjects not being interesting or challenging enough
- distractions
- lack of effort
- lack of concentration
- boredom
- unhappy and stressed teachers
- lack of encouragement
- poor or absent relations with teachers
- lack of fun in the classroom
- disliked lessons
- not attending to the task
- overly strict teachers
- teachers talking too much
- a general lack of enjoyment and fulfilment in school work

These are the constructs provided by them and their questions would be designed to elucidate the interviewees' responses accordingly.

Interviewer: If you were studying underachievement what question would you ask students?

Subject 11: Why do you think they are underachieving.

Interviewer: So let me ask you that question.

Subject 11: Just either not interested in the subject or it's really easy which tends to be both because if it's really easy I'm not interested in it.

Interviewer: So if it's too easy or too hard it turns you off?

Subject 11: I don't have trouble with it being too hard.

Able Underachievers would advise interviewees to self-assess themselves about what they are doing (effort), what they are not doing (avoidance), how much ability they have, what their marks or grades are and the size of the gap between ability and marks or grades. They would ask Able Underachievers if they had a plan to do anything about the underachievement and, if so, how the plan was working. They wanted to know whether the plan was established alone or with the help of a teacher. They would be interested to hear about the difficulty level of tasks set by teachers.

Interpretation

The Able Underachievers were able to identify with the needs and the aspirations of the research interviewer and were able to derive their own perspectives on the subject. They were not inclined to challenge the relevance of the research. They all seemed interested in what they were being asked and in their replies. They held strong views about causation as can be seen by the vocabulary of their responses.

Questions for the reader

If you were setting out to better understand pupil underachievement in terms of both causation and possible remedies what would you be asking and how?

Would you want to interview teachers or the Able Underachievers about themselves?

Would you prefer just to spend time in schools observing the actual behaviour of these Able Underachievers and their teachers?

Who do you think are the really influential players here (Able Underachievers, teachers, peers, parents, siblings, etc.)?

Would you want to replicate a study such as this in your own school as an action research project?

Concluding thoughts

Where is the wisdom we have lost in knowledge? Where is the knowledge we have lost in information? (Eliot 1962: 107)

Where is the information we have lost in data? (Kelly 1999)

Knowledge is theory. We should be thankful if action of management is based on theory. Knowledge has temporal spread. Information is not knowledge. The world is drowning in information but is slow in acquisition of knowledge. There is no substitute for knowledge. (Deming 1993)

These are reminders that in the end we are left with something of the voices of Able Underachievers that has been imperfectly summarised in this text by the authors in this research project. It is likely that if a team of Able Underachievers had done the research themselves they might well have produced different findings and offered different recommendations. It is now the task of the reader to extract the wisdom (if any) and the knowledge from the responses we collected and the conclusions we offer.

The previous chapters have detailed many interventions and strategies that can be adopted by adults (especially teachers) to reverse or reduce the under-achievement of able pupils. In this final chapter we highlight ways that senior managers can introduce whole-school systems that influence underachievement, and we explore ways of empowering the Able Underachievers themselves to take responsibility for changing their own future. Our Able Underachievers might need to be persuaded that the best way to predict the future is to be involved in creating it. They need to recognise that in being actively involved collectively in looking at the issue of underachievement, they have something to gain personally. If they are serious about changing their ways in Year 10 and later going on to college or university then we would be optimistic that these pupils would be receptive to the ideas that follow.

We have now had an opportunity to reflect on what a cross-section of 26 Able Underachievers from 11 different secondary schools had to say about the causes of underachievement and what steps might be taken to do something constructive about the problem. Throughout the text, the authors have asked readers to consider their own position and their reactions to what they have read. As yet, we have not heard your opinions on these matters and can only conjecture that some of this is alarming to you and signals great waste in our schools. Can we afford this waste? You can, no doubt, guess our concerns but for the record we state here what we as researchers think needs to be addressed.

The dominant theme to 'jump out' of the transcripts was one of lost opportunity for Able Underachievers and for others at school such as the teachers and at least some of the other students whose progress is sometimes compromised by the actions of disruptive or disaffected Able Underachievers. If you look back to our earlier list of constructs from the published literature on able pupils (Table 1.1) you will not see any specific reference to missing or lost opportunities. At the conception of the research project we read widely and brainstormed a lot about what factors might play a major role in causing and maintaining low levels of achievement in some able pupils. We considered such factors as teachers, peer and family influences, personality attributes, moods, social conditions, resources, standards, expectations, etc.

We had not expected the Able Underachievers to be so vocal in their identification of problems and solutions. Perhaps we anticipated that the investigation would be more complicated. With hindsight it now seems that the best intervention to recommend is to open up a dialogue between the Able Underachievers who might be willing to come forward and those teachers interested in the prospect of positive change. Perhaps all that is required is a prompt, a venue, a means to solicit volunteers, some time, an agenda and a few goals and ground rules to increase the probability of all parties being heard. It might help to keep it simple.

It would be fitting in this particular chapter to place the greatest responsibility on the Able Underachievers as the key players if they are to begin to realise their potential, in terms of both substantially improving their learning environments and raising their attainments. It would be easy to suggest that everyone else 'do something' constructive, but that would not involve the Able Underachievers adequately from the start and we suspect they might well just continue to opt out as the interventions had been invented and implemented by adults. To create the right climate for such a dialogue with Able Underachievers in schools, senior managers might begin by reflecting on what school systems are already in place to recognise the needs of pupils and teachers that influence achievement.

Teacher tasks

Before moving on to what Able Underachievers could be doing, let us suggest a few tasks that could and should perhaps be undertaken by adults such as the readers of this book who we hope will include classroom teachers, head teachers and able pupil coordinators. School staff could begin by using a checklist approach (see Table 6.1) to debate their strengths and weaknesses in promoting achievement.

The adults' first task would be to communicate the message to the Able Underachievers that their voices are being heard, taken seriously and believed, and that their concerns will be addressed in an appropriate manner. Adults could stress that a process has been started and that they want to hear more and will take steps to ensure that they do hear more. They want to promote a long-overdue dialogue and debate. They are willing to be good role models in starting conversations with Able Underachievers. They want to be more inclusive.

All that is required is a booked room and suitable invitations to the intended audience. Creating this forum might well be the single most important contribution that teachers can make. If the forum is to demonstrate dynamic, facilitative interaction, then, ideally, it ought to clearly demonstrate that it has the positive attributes that the Able Underachievers have said they value and ought not to show signs of the negative attributes that they tell us they dislike. This might require a little social engineering. The forum needs to be a safe place where people do not get punished for being too revolutionary or for giving honest feedback, and where unique, divergent learning and thinking styles and preferences are

Table 6.1 Checklist for schools: identifying existing good practice and priority areas for promoting achievement

Senior managers	
1	Does our school have an able pupil coordinator or designated member of staff to promote the needs of able pupils?
2	Does our school have an able pupil policy?
3	Do meetings exist in which Able Underachievers are represented to debate ways of promoting achievement?
4	Do heads of department make available provision in the form of extension (in-class differentiation) and enrichment (beyond the National Curriculum) activities in their subject areas?
5	Do mechanisms in school exist to address organisational stress and to promote emotional literacy?
Able pupil coordinators	
1	Are there mechanisms in school for identifying Able Achievers and Able Underachievers and for making deliberate efforts to promote collaboration between these groups?
2	Are Able Underachievers, including some pupils with SEN, pupils from ethnic minorities and those from poor socio-economic backgrounds, included in school provision for able pupils?
3	Does our school promote links with the local community (parents, other schools, higher education establishments and local businesses) to help develop a network of support and motivation for able pupils?
4	Is there a mechanism in school for discovering pupils' talents and interests and using them to promote collaboration and motivation?
5	Does our school have a mentoring system for Able Underachievers?
6	Have staff in our school had access to training on teaching and learning styles and on how to plan to meet the needs of able pupils?
Classroom teachers	
1	Do individual teachers meet with Able Underachievers (and also their parents) out of class to consult with them about possibilities for improving their performance?
2	Do teachers make use of peer observation or self-assessment to reflect on the quality of their explanations and the way they question pupils?
3	Do individual teachers work in socially responsive classrooms (by allowing some pupil talk, discussion, peer and group work)?
4	Do teachers make use of observations to determine 'how a pupil is being intelligent' and how they learn best and use these observations to identify able pupils and to modify their teaching style to address pupil preferences?
5	Do teachers make good use of creative and practical approaches across subject areas?
6	Do individual teachers challenge able pupils to think at different levels and to engage in more synthesis (creative thinking) and evaluation (giving opinions and explanations of these opinions)?
7	Do teachers promote effective use of study skills in their subject area (e.g. the use of mind maps)?
8	Do teachers try to take a personal interest in Able Underachievers?
9	Are pupils encouraged to keep learning logs to reflect on the way in which they approach tasks and their emotional response to learning?

acknowledged and valued. If Able Underachievers show imagination, creativity, spontaneity and action, these need to be conspicuously reinforced by adults so as to increase the possibility of greater involvement among the Able Underachievers, who might well initially see this dialogue as risky or suspicious.

A lot of thought could go into creating the right environment or climate on arrival. The audience would need to be 'warmed up' with reasonable expectations as to how this initial meeting will be different from sitting in class listening to an adult talk. A huge audience is not required. The early stages could work effectively with just a few committed volunteers (adults and pupils).

If adults 'get it right', the talents of these pupils ought to blossom in this type of setting. If the student contributions are met with positive regard and respect and are not publicly greeted with scepticism or harsh judgements we can hope to hear more from them, as this research has shown. We would begin to tap into underused resources among the Able Underachiever population and see how they could make a contribution to introducing constructive changes in the school environment instead of attacking it, whether actively or passively.

From the beginning, Able Underachievers ought to feel that something unique and special and real is actually happening in their school as a direct result of this challenge. As such, we would hope that they would become more intrinsically motivated to effect personal change. Staff also ought to perceive that new energy, new ideas and new people resources are on the table for consideration and possible use. Potentially everyone can win from this arrangement. As the forum matures it is likely that someone will identify other subgroups beyond Able Underachievers within school that are under-represented and whose voices and contributions might well be sought in the hopes of furthering the inclusive nature of the school community via fresh research.

Adults could be pupil advocates supporting change that would be in everyone's interest. They could create the opportunities, the time and the place for important conversations to begin, mostly involving Able Underachievers, teachers, peers and parents. They could agree to work to sell innovation, remove obstacles, overcome resistance and promote the voices of Able Underachievers when necessary. This is not deemed to be an easy task but the rewards for any school community wanting to raise standards will be enormous.

We strongly believe that these adult–pupil conversations could inspire local research which will lead to interventions that will boost the productivity of Able Underachievers. However, if readers still need convincing about other interventions, then here are some further empowering suggestions to hold in reserve:

- quality feedback involving dialogue about shortcomings with written work submitted and how the pupil thinks he or she could have been done better, given in a tutorial setting;
- more appropriate target setting for homework with follow-up evaluation;
- well-equipped homework centres in the community when home circumstances are less than ideal, open perhaps for longer hours than normal;
- reduced distractions;
- soliciting constructive feedback from pupils about tasks deemed boring, unchallenging or inappropriate;
- attention to diet, exercise and sleep as background factors;
- time management, organisational, research and study skills training;
- pupil/parent resource packs including organisations and website addresses;
- access for able pupils to attend Saturday classes and summer schools;
- hotlines for Able Underachievers who need support with homework;
- analyses of learning environments, looking at noise, seating, room temperature, crowding, partitions, refreshments and better facilities for short breaks;
- more visible celebration of pupil achievements;
- innovative National Curriculum citizenship and leadership training activities;
- Able Underachievers being regrouped (where possible) into Able Achiever sets;
- talent spotting among the non-conforming Able Underachievers;
- staff support programmes to recognise and reduce the incidence of stress at school.

Able Underachiever tasks

It must be accepted that educational innovations for Able Underachievers will be gradual and staged for a variety of reasons. At present these pupils are not asking for extra chores. They will need some convincing. The research quoted previously in this book demonstrates that Able Underachievers have lots of abilities and can constructively refrain from blaming all of their problems with underachievement onto others. This is the positive news. However, on the negative side, Able Underachievers do not at present feel they own the problem of underachievement or all the responsibility for reducing it. They will probably need some diplomatic convincing about potential new responsibilities, which is where the adults as stakeholders probably hold the keys to getting these new conversations started.

Let us imagine that the Able Underachievers, their teachers (and possibly a sample of parents) in a particular secondary school are given the opportunity to read this book or a summary of it. They are then invited to an initial school forum to participate in discussions about the main issues from a local perspective.

Imagine what might happen if all the participants had thought about the ideas in this book and reflected on and responded to the questions that are presented from time to time. What if those assembled debated the text thoroughly, found fault with some aspects of this book and decided to conduct their own background local research, perhaps with Able Underachievers and teachers working in pairs? They could write out their own questions based on local circumstances and a desire to produce a more appropriate mechanism to discover the real thoughts, attitudes, behaviours and beliefs among all the stakeholders in the community.

They might decide to interview individuals such as other Able Underachievers, Able Achievers, other pupils, teachers, administrators, parents, advisers, governors, careers officers, employers, school leavers, excluded pupils, educational psychologists, etc. They might want to work with focus groups or use questionnaire or observation methods to broaden the methodology of the local research that might inform subsequent decision making. They certainly ought to feel a sense of pride in this research. If they lacked adequate research methodology training this could be offered where necessary and where desired.

The act of engaging in local educational research has pedagogical value in its own right and neatly fits into the Department for Education and Skills' new interest in teaching citizenship in schools. The results could be published and debated, especially when the research points to real school-based innovations that have popular support. Once published, local action research findings would provide the community with a new type of information that previously was neither collected nor debated.

Local research would provide evidence for those who perhaps might have thought they were in a minority position. One outcome could be to hold an annual student–teacher day in which the student body takes over the roles of all school staff for a day under the supervision of existing school staff. The procedure could then be made subject to an evaluation exercise to demonstrate its merits and what could be done to make it even more effective during the next year. Another outcome might be to identify the barriers to higher achievement and establish responsibility (pupil, teacher, parent or shared) to put in place an action plan to improve standards.

The overall purpose of the research exercise is to convince stakeholders, and especially the Able Underachievers, that the debate is open and that all voices will be heard. The work would be designed to do something about the missing communication that we have seen highlighted in the research reported in this book. All parties would be given an opportunity to talk about underachievement and what could be done about it.

Those attending these meetings could wrestle with the notion of problem identification and, more importantly, *problem ownership* and responsibility. At least some Able Underachiever participants might be surprised to hear both some teachers and some Able Underachievers stating that Able Underachievers owned a share of the problem. This could be real personal learning. By owning a share in the problem you increase the chances of being able to do something positive about it. It can be empowering. It would also be fascinating to hear more cynical Able Underachievers distancing themselves from the underachievement phenomenon and wanting to blame teachers. They might well be challenged. Has this opportunity for communication taken place previously?

We should look for a reduction in both apathy and powerlessness if the discussions realise their full potential. It could raise the tone and the expectations of the forum type meetings. Of course, some might find this process too revolutionary in that students could actually be calling for more evaluation of teaching lessons and more accountability. The teachers would have to address this or be accused of 'playing at teaching democracy' when in reality some might really not want to see the student body becoming empowered and finding its voice. In essence, some people attending the forum may need to be prepared to hear what they do not want to hear.

The outcome that would excite us would be to hear the voices of the previously mostly silent Able Underachievers (who perhaps had opted out) joining the potentially more outspoken and confident Able Achievers in presenting some long-overdue social leadership within schools. What an alliance! It could easily double the strength and the volume of the student perspective at a time when we have some good evidence that people are not effectively communicating or sharing perspectives in schools. Some pupils could actually be talking more like adults within a more adult-type learning context.

The overall outcome could be to create a more responsive school environment that is more cohesive, cooperative and vibrant. The school could benefit from the use of a consultative feedback loop so that teachers regularly hear what their students think about the way lessons are conducted, an established practice in higher education where it seems to work. How often do we see it occurring in secondary schools?

Successful governments, public services, industries and businesses are now bending over backwards to communicate effectively and conspicuously with their stakeholders so as to appear to be 'listening organisations' responsive to the needs of the public, the users, the consumers, the rate payers, etc. They take feedback very seriously and do this in a conspicuous manner. They set up procedures to address complaints and find ways of resolving problems that really work. They create and listen to focus groups as a way of anticipating demands and problems long before they actually surface. They actively seek to know everything possible about their organisation, warts and all. The best organisations are less reliant on outsiders such as inspectors and auditors because their own internal self-evaluation procedures are so effective. These procedures often involve staff who work within a supportive host culture and who have access to quality supervision that supports these values and reduces unnecessary organisational stress (Scaife 2001; Hawkins and Shohet 1989).

Could this change in seeking active feedback apply in schools? Who could set it up? We would argue that these issues about consultation with participants such as the Able Underachievers could be raised by any stakeholder in the education business, provided an appropriate forum was in operation such as the one suggested above in which Able Underachievers and others are engaging in facilitative communications with one another. Able Underachievers could offer a unique perspective that perhaps has not been effectively heard in the past, if the opinions solicited in the earlier research prove valid across a wider sampling of pupils. Again we want to stress that our study was based on a relatively small sample and that further evidence needs to be gathered to corroborate these findings on a wider scale.

Think of the advantages in the time saved if the vast bulk of the Able Underachiever subgroup was productively working, instead of engaging in counterproductive activities such as sabotaging lessons and occupying more than a fair share of school pastoral time with their misbehaviour. Think of all the additional people resources that would be released if there was less of the 'cat and mouse game' because the motivation for the game no longer applied.

There was a time when workers in automobile assembly factories went to great efforts recreationally to conceal an inappropriate spare part in a vehicle so as not to be caught by an inspector until the car almost rolled off the assembly line and the perpetrator could not be traced. This was the 'cat and mouse game' at its peak within industry. We suspect that when workers and management finally opened a dialogue, they all agreed that the energy going into sabotage and detection was not in the best interests of all the players. It actually drained energy and people resources away from long-term goals. Their competitors had found more constructive games to play and were actually winning in a commercial sense by making vehicles less expensively than those playing the sabotage game.

Some of the outdated traditional teaching practices could recede into history or at least hold a lower profile. The ratio of teacher-talk to pupil-talk could be altered in favour of pupils. There might be less wasted teacher energy going into crowd control and maintaining silence. Students could be questioned about their perceptions of changes in school. The ultimate goals would be to see higher productivity among Able Underachievers and less criticism that their teachers are not responsive to constructive criticism.

Able Underachievers could feel a greater sense of pride in school life because the innovations would have come at least in part from their own research and not simply been set up by teachers. There is an expression 'NGIE' which stands for 'No good . . . invented elsewhere'. It highlights the predictable problems when someone tries to be directive and prescribe too much to a client group. Innovations work best when stakeholders feel intuitively some deeper sense of authorship in the procedures and the products.

If someone (a teacher, an Able Underachiever, a parent, a governor or perhaps even an outsider) simply provides the seeds or whatever it takes to help the communication process get started in just a few schools we would be happy to step back and watch the process. Changes could take place in many different ways but that would not suggest a fault in the foregoing argument. It would merely validate some of what we have heard in the voices of these Able Underachievers.

Not to hear this discussion and debate would simply be another lost opportunity. This communicating forum (where the conversations that have not been happening spontaneously now show potential) seems like the principal contribution coming out of this study. It leaves Able Underachievers and potentially all the other stakeholders, such as teachers, parents and peers, with the tasks of doing research and devising individual or collective interventions.

If Able Underachievers are still looking for a menu of suggestions before joining a forum or embarking on their own research, the following provisional list is offered. Many of the suggestions came from those people consulted during the research and some were offered with considerable enthusiasm and indeed pride:

- take some responsible risks;
- overcome obstacles;
- regain opportunity;
- lose the script that says these ideas are impossible;
- seek more facilitative conversations with teachers and parents;
- find similar voices to your own ('like minds');
- own the problem or at least part of it;
- be more optimistic;
- be more active and less passive at school;
- be an ally to a teacher who is experiencing trouble with a lesson (make an offer);
- seek allies such as peers, teachers, mentors, parents, siblings, advocates, etc.;
- use drama, role training and challenge the stereotypes surrounding Able Achievers;
- seek student government and exercise your rights;
- use social and linguistic skills to persuade others such as teachers, peers and parents;
- set higher standards and appropriate self-targets;
- suggest a Circle of Friends for someone at school who is unnecessarily isolated;
- initiate anti-bullying tactics when Able Achievers are teased;
- do something social with an Able Achiever and find common interests;
- celebrate your successes and those of others;
- break habits that are counterproductive;
- try harder to get your own personal needs met;
- assert yourself;
- get out of the rut (*status quo*);
- debate the merits of a delayed gratification pattern; and
- find incentives to work harder.

Parent tasks

We can provide some additional suggestions that were inspired by the spirit of the interviews, again using the theme of lost opportunities. We were worried that some parents might feel marginalised and want to know what else they might be able to offer that might stimulate their Able Underachievers to try harder at school work. What could these parents and their teenagers do regularly together to move beyond just having facilitative conversations such as those recommended for teachers and pupils in previous chapters?

Purposeful collaboration could involve any of the following:

- working on a PC and surfing the Internet;
- building or repairing something;
- playing music together, for example in a band or orchestra;
- participating in a local dramatic event;
- doing voluntary work together in the community;
- planning field trips, for example to museums, observatories, galleries, factories, theatres, cinemas, studios, laboratories, universities, foreign countries;
- engaging in recreational activity with a training element such as camping, running, walking, skating, trekking or assisting on an archaeological dig;
- attending the local leisure centre either for training (getting fit together) or as members of a team;
- working together on a political task or as members of a church or religious group;
- starting the long-overdue conversation about these issues with young people that has not yet happened spontaneously; and
- working and learning alongside each other and with each other.

Some students have access to these types of family activities and some take advantage of them, while others reject these activities, preferring to spend free time with their peers. Some resistance might be overcome if friends were asked to participate as well.

The thin edge of the wedge

The above proposals do not need to be embraced in their entirety. They are offered as a starting point like a menu in a restaurant. If individual schools start the process of organising a meeting or a forum after school or in an evening session, and if some modest local participatory research results, then some organisational change is inevitable. Each school will then find its own level and tolerance for change at an appropriate pace.

In the end, it is up to the wider community to decide what it wants and exactly how it chooses to celebrate its transitions and its innovations, and how it overcomes inertia, fear and resistance. We wish you luck and would like to hear of your progress.

Appendix 1

Staged criteria for the selection of Able Underachievers

Stage 1: In Year 7 the pupil scored 115 or better on the non-verbal Cognitive Abilities Test (CAT).

This task asked schools to look back at the CAT testing data collected when the current Year 9 pupils were in Year 7. This procedure should have selected a pool of those pupils who on entry to secondary education in Year 7 would have been considered (using this criterion alone) to have above average potential. It could have failed to select highly creative pupils who do not do well on tests but who have good ability otherwise. It was the starting point to find pupils with ability, using a relatively standardised but far from perfect procedure.

Head teachers (HTs) responded to this invitation with enthusiasm although there were some problems with the CAT score criterion which was included as a safeguard. Basically, we wanted to use multiple selection criteria to avoid interviewing candidates who might not be particularly able but just appeared to be so to the teachers. Unfortunately, some HTs either did not have the CAT data (as with a pupil transferring into the LEA from a school that did not use CAT tests), or felt inclined to select candidates slightly below the 115 standardised score. Those with missing CAT data were omitted at this stage. In a few cases the cut-off figure might have dropped to 112. Rather than discard the candidate he or she was included in the Stage 1 pool of candidates as planned.

Stage 2: The staff would describe the pupil as an Able Underachiever.

From the list of pupils produced in Stage 1 the staff then reselected a smaller group or subset based on the additional criterion which was, essentially, staff nominations. If staff disagreed with any nominations at Stage 1, feeling that the non-verbal test was not a good predictor of academic talent or was wrong, these pupils could be omitted at this stage. Staff were not asked to nominate pupils outside of the Stage 1 list.

Stage 3: The parents would agree that the pupil is an Able Underachiever.

The Stage 2 list was then further reduced by asking schools to ascertain that parents (or carers) were in basic agreement that their son or daughter was an Able Underachiever. If the parent(s) objected to either the selection procedure or the interview invitation for their son or daughter, the pupil in question was dropped from the selection list. We probably lost some genuine Able Underachievers here because their parents were denying or minimising the problems with underachievement. This could well have reduced the size of the pool from which final interviewees were chosen.

Stage 4: The pupil himself or herself agrees that he or she is underachieving at school.
This last stage sought confirmation from the target pupil that he or she agreed with
the above findings and was willing to undergo an interview at school. By this means
we probably lost non-volunteers who either did not want to assist us or were
denying the extent of their underachievement.

A random selection from the list of Able Underachievers who survived the four-
stage screening procedure was then made.

To some extent we were asking school staff to nominate candidates from a pre-
selected list and to do this informed by the process of using a widely accepted
testing procedure at Stage 1. Undoubtedly there were some Able Underachievers
who fell through this net (false negatives) and were not selected, such as someone
absent on the day of testing or recently achieving at a much higher level
academically, although only on a very temporary basis. Likewise we might well have
captured a very small number of pupils (false positives) who were not really genuine
Able Underachievers but just looked that way to the teachers making the selections.
Teachers are subject to all sorts of possible error in making judgements, but
remember that the list of pupils seen by school staff had all done well at Stage 1.

By using a four-stage selection model and then randomly choosing a subset of
these, we hopefully found a sample to interview who were most likely to be
authentic Able Underachievers. With greater study and effort we probably could
have refined the method and, therefore, been more precise in obtaining genuine
Year 9 volunteer Able Underachievers to interview. That task could be left for
another day or another team of researchers. We would welcome this.

In the end, we decided to interview a small number of Year 9 Able
Underachiever pupils from each of 11 randomly chosen schools. The range was
from one to four in each school.

Appendix 2

Transcripts and the use of a grounded theory approach by means of ATLAS.ti

All the 26 tape recordings were transcribed and stored as *MS Word* files. A cross-section of them were checked for transcription accuracy and were found to be very good reproductions of what was said in the interviews. There were very few instances when the typist was unable to transcribe what was said and this inevitably was caused by background noise, for example when bells were ringing in schools and the volume of noisy conversation outside the interview room increased. When it was really intrusive, the interviews were temporarily interrupted.

Subsequently, the 26 *Word* format transcripts were converted into narrower text files with line breaks to facilitate importing into the ATLAS.ti software for qualitative analysis.

Importing the 26 narrow transcripts into the ATLAS.ti software application, with each containing dialogue associated with the 36 key items with follow-up questions, enables the user to analyse the resulting matrix of text or prose. In summary, the entire set of transcripts contains over 65,000 words. Each word belongs to one of 936 cells formed by the cross-section of 26 subjects by 36 questions. This averages about 70 words in each cell. This is considerably more data than, for example, might be obtained using a quantitative approach, such as a multiple choice questionnaire.

If readers want more information about ATLAS.ti software and its author (Muhr 1997) they can visit the ATLAS.ti website [http://www.atlasti.de/index.html] and download a trial version of the software for demonstration purposes. This will allow the reader to see sample screen shots that may facilitate interpretation of what follows.

Coding quotations

With the text in the left-hand panel on the screen, the user can create visible codes in the right-hand panel alongside the associated text. This is usually done by selecting or highlighting the text that one wants to code. There are many coding techniques but for now let us take a simple example. On the left of the screen is the dialogue that is both Question 1 and the first interviewee's responses to it. This text can be selected in its entirety and given the code of 1. In future, if the user ever needs to get back to this particular textual quotation, it can be easily found.

All 26 transcripts were carefully read and coded by the same interviewer. Eventually, over 200 codes were generated for this textual archive. By employing the codes, the user can systematically retrieve the highlighted quotation associated with any individual code or a combination of codes. Effectively, all 65,000 words are surveyed and codes are applied to those words that are selected where the user might want to get back to them at a later date.

Initial use of coding

The first analyses performed focused on having ATLAS.ti produce a summary of all the highlighted quotations stored against each of the codes 1–36 which were used to identify the semi-structured questions. For example, it was an easy task to get ATLAS.ti to generate paper output of all the text transcribed that was associated with Question 1. These operations were performed for all 36 questions and this facilitated the textual analysis.

Later, the text was further analysed using codes that were either part of the pupils' voices or were abstractions created by the researchers. Some examples of codes we used were 'boredom', 'cadets', 'shouting' and 'lost opportunity'.

For comparative purporses, one author did all the coding using ATLAS.ti while the other independently did all the coding by hand using highlighter in the traditional grounded theory manner. This allowed us to compare findings, debate interpretations and then draft the chapters of this book as an integrated and cooperative project.

References

Adey, P. and Shayer, M. (1994) *Really Raising Standards: Cognitive intervention and academic achievement.* London: Routledge.

Adey, P .S., Shayer, M. and Yates, C. (1989) *Thinking Science: The curriculum materials of the CASE Project.* London: Thomas Nelson and Sons.

Ajmal, Y. and Rees, I. (eds) (2001) *Solutions in Schools: Creative applications of solution focused brief thinking with young people and adults.* London: BT Press.

Alderman, M. K. (1990) 'Motivation for at-risk students'. *Educational Leadership*, 48, 27–30.

Allwright, D. (1986) 'Making sense of instruction', workshop presentation, RELC Regional Seminar, Singapore, April, cited in Nunan, D. (1989) *Understanding Language Classrooms.* Hemel Hempstead: Prentice-Hall.

Ashman, A. and Conway, R. (1993) *Using Cognitive Methods in the Classroom.* London: Routledge.

Bailey, S. (2000) 'Culturally diverse gifted students', in Stopper, M. J. (ed.) *Meeting the Social and Emotional Needs of Gifted and Talented Children.* London: David Fulton Publishers.

Baker, C. (2000) 'Out of the kitchen with Gary Rhodes', *Vivid*, 4, 36–7.

Bandura, A. and Schunk, D. (1981) 'Cultivating competence, self-efficacy and intrinsic interest through proximal self motivation', *Journal of Personality and Social Psychology*, 41, 885–98.

Bloom, B. S. (1976) *Taxonomy of Educational Objectives. Vol. 1.* London: Longman.

Bouchard, L. (1995) 'Ways to increase creativity', Council for Gifted Children World Conference, Hong Kong.

Brown, G. and Armstrong, S. (1984) 'Explaining and explanations', in Wragg, E. C. (ed.) *Classroom Teaching Skills.* London: Croom Helm.

Brown, G. and Hatton, N. (1982) *Explanations and Explaining: A teaching skills workbook.* London: Macmillan.

Brown, G. and Wragg, E. C. (1993) *Questioning.* London: Routledge.

Burden, R. L. (1994) 'Trends and developments in educational psychology – an international perspective', *School Psychology International*, 15 (4), 293–347.

Butler-Por, N. (1987) *Underachievers in School: Issues and intervention.* Chichester: John Wiley and Sons.

Buzan, T. (1993) *The Mind Map Book.* London: BBC Books.

Canter, L. and Canter, M. (1992) *Lee Canter's Assertive Discipline: Positive behaviour management for today's classroom.* Santa Monica CA: Canter and Associates.

Carnegie Council on Adolescent Development (1989) *Turning Points: Preparing American youth for the 21st century.* Washington DC: Carnegie Council on Adolescent Development.

Cheshire County Council (1996) *Cheshire Management Guidelines – Identifying and providing for our most able pupils.* Chester: Cheshire County Council Education Services.

Covington, M. V. (1992) *Making the Grade – A self worth perspective on motivation and school reform.* Cambridge: Cambridge University Press.

Crystal, D. (1987) *The Cambridge Encyclopaedia of Language.* Cambridge: Cambridge University Press.

Csikszentmihalyi, M. Rathunde, K. and Whalen, S. (1997) *Talented Teenagers – The roots of success and failure.* Cambridge: Cambridge University Press.

de Bono, E. (1999) *New Thinking for the New Millennium.* London: Viking.

Deci, E. (1988) 'Intrinsic motivation and gifted learners', 10th International Bulgarian Symposium on Education, Plovdiv. October.

Deci, E. L., Nezlek, J. and Sheinman, L. (1981) 'Characteristics of the rewards and intrinsic motivation of the rewardee', *Journal of Personality and Social Psychology*, 40, 1–10.

Deming, W. E. (1993) *The New Economics.* Cambridge, Massachusetts: MIT Press.

DfEE National Advisory Committee on Creative and Cultural Education (1999) *All Our Futures: Creativity, culture and education.* London: DfEE.

DfES (2001) *Key Stage 3 National Pilot on Teaching and Learning in the Foundation Subjects.* London: DfES Publications.

Dweck, C. (1975) 'The role of expectations and attributions in the alleviation of learned helplessness', *Journal of Personality and Social Psychology*, 31, 674–685.

Eliot, T. S. (1962) 'Choruses from the rock', *Selected Poems*, NY: Harvest Harcourt.

Eyre, D. (1997) *Able Children in Ordinary Schools.* London: David Fulton Publishers.

Feuerstein, R. (1973) 'The role of cultural transmission in the development of intelligence. Allan Bronfman Lecture, Quebec, Canada, September 1973, cited in Sharron, H. and Coulter, M. (1994) *Changing Children's Minds.* Birmingham: The Sharron Publishing Company.

Feuerstein, R., Rand, Y., Hoffman, M. and Miller, M. (1980) *Instrumental Enrichment: An intervention programme for cognitive modifiability.* Baltimore, MD: University Park Press.

Fisher, R. (1996) *Stories for Thinking.* Oxford: Nash Pollock.

Flanders, N. (1970) *Analysing Classroom Behaviour.* New York: Addison-Wesley.

Freeman, J. (1996) *Highly Able Girls and Boys.* London: DfEE.

Freeman, J. (1997) 'The emotional development of the highly able', *European Journal of Psychology in Education*, XII, 479–93.

Freire, P. (1970) *Pedagogy of the Oppressed*. New York: Continuum.

Gagne, R. L. (1973) *The Essentials of Learning*. London: Holt, Rinehart and Winston.

Gagne, R. L. (1991) 'Toward a differentiated model of giftedness and talent' in Colangelo, N. and Davis, G. A. (eds) *Handbook of Gifted Education*. Boston: Allyn and Bacon.

Gardner, H. (1993) *Frames of Mind: The theory of multiple intelligences* (2nd edn). London: Fontana-Collins.

George, D. (1992) *The Challenge of the Able Child*. London: David Fulton Publishers.

Goleman, D. (1996) *Emotional Intelligence*. London: Bloomsbury.

Gomme, S. (2000) 'The Role of the Family' in Stopper, M. J. (ed.) *Meeting the Social and Emotional Needs of Gifted and Talented Children*. London: David Fulton Publishers.

Gross, M. U. M. (1994) 'Responding to the social and emotional needs of gifted children', *Australian Journal of Gifted Children*, 3(2), 4–10.

Hartmann, T. (1998) *Healing ADD*. California: Underwood Books.

Hawkins, P. and Shohet, R. (1989) *Supervision in the Helping Professions* (2nd edn). Milton Keynes: Open University Press.

House of Commons, Education and Employment Committee (1999) *Highly Able Children*. London: The Stationery Office.

Hulmes, E. (1998) *Education and Cultural Diversity*. London: Longman.

Hymer, B. (2000) 'Understanding and overcoming underachievement in boys', in Montgomery, D. (ed.) *Able Underachievers*. London: Whurr Publishers.

Kellmer-Pringle, M. (1970) *Able Misfits*. London: Longman.

Kelly, D. (1999) Personal communication.

Kerry, T. (1983) *Finding and Helping the Able Child*. London: Croom Helm.

Kyriacou, C. (1991) *Essential Teaching Skills*. Hemel Hempstead: Simon and Schuster Education.

Lake, M. (1989) 'Mind games in Milton Keynes', *Special Children*, February 1989, 20–3.

Lawrence, D. (1999) *Teaching with Confidence – A guide to enhancing teacher self-esteem Primary Schools*. London: Paul Chapman Publishing.

Leyden, S. (1985) *Helping the Child of Exceptional Ability*. London: Croom Helm.

Leyden, S. and Bennett, D. (1995) 'Why not talk to the pupils?' *Flying High*, Spring 1995, 25–7.

Lipman, M., Sharp A. U., Oscanyan, Frederick S. (1980) *Philosophy in the Classroom*. Philadelphia: Temple University Press

Locke A. and Beech, M. (1991) *Teaching Talking*. Windsor: NFER-Nelson.

Maslow, A. (1954) *Motivation and Personality*. New York: Harper and Row.

Miles, M. B. and Huberman, A. M. (1994) *Qualitative Data Analysis – A source book of new methods*. London: Sage Publications.

Montgomery, D. (1984) *Evaluation and Enhancement of Teaching Performance*. Maldon: Learning Difficulties Research Project.

Montgomery, D. (1999) *Positive Appraisal through Classroom Observation*. London: David Fulton Publishers.

Montgomery, D. (2000) 'Combating literacy difficulties in able achievers', in Montgomery, D. (ed.) (2000) *Able Underachievers*. London: Whurr Publishers.

Morgan, N. and Saxton, J. (1991) *Teaching, Questioning and Learning*. London: Routledge.

Muhr, T. (1997) ATLAS.ti: *The Knowledge Workbench.* London: Scolari.

Nottinghamshire County Council (2000) *Able Pupils – Providing for able pupils and those with exceptional talent.* Nottinghamshire County Council Education.

Nunan, D. (1989) *Understanding Language Classrooms.* Hertfordshire: Prentice-Hall.

O'Grady, A. L. (1995) 'The onset of academic underachievement among gifted adolescents: causal attributions and the perceived effect of early interventions', Ph.D. dissertation. The University of Connecticut.

Ogilvie, E. (1973) *Gifted Children in Primary Schools.* London: Macmillan.

Passow, A. H. (1990) 'Needed research and development in teaching high ability children', *European Journal of High Ability,* 1, 15–24.

Perkins, D. N. (2002) Personal communication.

Picozzo, R. (1982) 'Gifted underachievers', *Roeper Review,* 4, 18–21.

Pomerantz, K. A. (2000) 'Profile of language use – Adult' (unpublished).

Redding, R. E. (1989) 'Underachievement in the verbally gifted: implications for pedagogy', *Psychology in the Schools,* 26, 275–91.

Renzulli, J.S. (1986) 'The three ring conception of giftedness: a developmental model for creative productivity', in Sternberg, R. J. and Davidson, J. H. (eds) *Conceptions of Giftedness,* 53–93, Cambridge: Cambridge University Press.

Roeders, P. (1995) 'Student-assisted education – the active way of differentiation in the classroom: basic concepts and effects', paper presented at the European Seminar of ECHA, Antwerp, April, cited in Montgomery, D. (2000) 'Inclusive education for able underachievers: changing teaching for learning', in Montgomery, D. (ed.) *Able Underachievers.* London: Whurr Publishers.

Romaine, S. (1984) *The Language of Children and Adolescents.* Oxford: Basil Blackwell.

Sadler, K. (2000a) 'The needs of able pupils' (unpublished).

Sadler, K. (2000b) 'Attributors and solutions for the underachievement of able pupils', *Educating Able Children,* 4(1).

Scaife, J. (2001) *Supervision in the Mental Health Professions: A practitioner's guide.* Hove, East Sussex: Brunner-Routledge.

Schmitz, C. C. and Galbraith, J. (1985) M*anaging the Social and Emotional Needs of the Gifted.* Minneapolis: Free Spirit Publishing.

Sharp, P. (2001) *Nurturing Emotional Literacy.* London: David Fulton Publishers.

Smith, P., Cowie, H. and Blades, M. (1998) *Understanding Children's Development* (3rd edn). Oxford: Blackwell Publishers.

Sternberg, R. J. (1997) *Thinking Styles.* Cambridge: Cambridge University Press.

Sternberg R. J. and Davidson, J. E. (1986) *Conceptions of Giftedness.* Cambridge: Cambridge University Press.

Stopper, M. J. (2000) (ed.) *Meeting the Social and Emotional Needs of Gifted and Talented Children.* London: David Fulton Publishers.

Strauss, A. L. and Corbin, J. (1998) *Basics of Qualitative Research: Techniques and procedures for developing grounded theory.* (2nd edn). London: Sage.

Supplee, P. L. (1990) *Reaching the Gifted Underachiever: Program strategy and Design.* New York: Teachers College Press.

Teare, B. (1997) *Effective Provision for Able and Talented Pupils.* Network Educational

Press.

Topping, K. J. (1988) *The Peer Tutoring Handbook.* London: Croom Helm.

Tough, J. (1979) *Talk for Teaching and Learning.* London: Ward Locke.

Valsiner, J. and Leung, M. (1994) 'From intelligence to knowledge construction', in Sternberg, R. J. and Wagner, R. K. (eds) *Mind in Context.* Cambridge: Cambridge University Press.

Vygotsky, L. S. (1962) *Thought and Language.* New York: Wiley.

Wallace, B. (2000) 'Able and talented learners from socio-economically disadvantaged communities', in Stopper, M. J. (ed.) *Meeting the Social and Emotional Needs of Gifted and Talented Children.* London: David Fulton Publishers.

West, T. G. (1991) *In the Mind's Eye: Visual thinkers, gifted people with learning difficulties, computer images and the ironies of creativity.* Buffalo, New York: Prometheus.

Wheldall, K. and Glynn, T. (1989) *Effective Classroom Learning.* Oxford: Blackwell.

Whitmore, J. R. (1980) *Giftedness, Conflict and Underachievement.* Boston, MA: Allyn and Bacon, Inc.

Whitmore, J. R. (1985) 'New challenges to common identification practices', in Freeman, J. (ed.) *The Psychology of Gifted Children.* Chichester: Wiley.

Whybra, J. (2000) 'Extension and enrichment programmes: A place I could fit in', in Stopper, M. J. (ed.) *Meeting the Social and Emotional Needs of Gifted and Talented Children.* London: David Fulton Publishers.

Wilcockson, D. (1997) 'Underachievement in a middle school', *Education Today,* 47(1).

Wills, L. and Munro, J. (2000) 'Changing the teaching for the underachieving able child: The Ruyton School experience', in Montgomery, D. (ed.) *Able Underachievers.* London: Whurr Publishers.

Index